对 外 汉 语 本 科 系 列 教 材

语言技能类　　一年级教材

汉语口语教程

HANYU KOUYU JIAOCHENG

第一册

杨寄洲 贾永芬 编著

北京语言大学出版社
BEIJING LANGUAGE AND CULTURE UNIVERSITY PRESS

图书在版编目（CIP）数据

汉语口语教程．第一册 / 杨寄洲，贾永芬编著．--
北京 ：北京语言大学出版社，2022.8（2024.8 重印）
ISBN 978-7-5619-5930-5

Ⅰ.①汉… Ⅱ.①杨… ②贾… Ⅲ.①汉语－口语－
对外汉语教学－教材 Ⅳ.① H195.4

中国版本图书馆 CIP 数据核字（2021）第 163204 号

汉语口语教程 第一册

HANYU KOUYU JIAOCHENG DI-YI CE

责任编辑：王巧燕 赫 栗
排版制作：北京创艺涵文化发展有限公司
责任印制：周 燚

出版发行：北京语言大学出版社
社 址：北京市海淀区学院路 15 号，100083
网 址：www.blcup.com
电子信箱：service@blcup.com
电 话：编 辑 部 8610-82303647/3592/3724
国内发行 8610-82303650/3591/3648
海外发行 8610-82303365/3080/3668
北语书店 8610-82303653
网购咨询 8610-82303908
印 刷：北京富资园科技发展有限公司

版 次：2022 年 8 月第 1 版　　印 次：2024 年 8 月第 3 次印刷
开 本：787 毫米 × 1092 毫米 1/16　　印 张：10
字 数：161 千字
定 价：49.00 元

PRINTED IN CHINA
凡有印装质量问题，本社负责调换。QQ：1367565611，电话：010-82303590

前言

《汉语口语教程》是为零起点的汉语学习者编写的口语教材，适用于开展学历教育和非学历教育以及各类国际汉语教育的教学单位。

本教程的编写理念是：力求培养学生成才。

选择学习汉语的外国学生，尤其是来华学习汉语的留学生大多处于人生的最佳年龄段，他们万里迢迢来到中国，来到我们身边，追求自己的人生梦想，跟我们学习汉语，我们不能辜负了他们。我们一定要树立培养学生成才的理念，哪怕学生只学一年半载，也要为他们今后的发展着想。

口语课是单项技能训练课。

如果说听力课和阅读课重在输入的话，那么口语课则重在输出。这就要求学生在课堂上要尽可能多地开口说话，要求教师要借助教材，调动和利用一切教学手段和技巧，激发学生的表达欲望。师生之间、生生之间要开展接近实际的交际会话，培养、操练学生的口头表达能力。要让学生通过一年的学习，能够运用汉语满足日常交际需要，并为他们升入高年级或进入其他专业学习（如学医、学工等）打下一个良好的基础。

口语课堂应是师生互动、演示教材的“剧场”。

我们希望，任课教师一定要充分利用课堂，充分利用师生面对面的语境，指导并共同进行师生之间、生生之间的交际会话。课堂交际会话当然是模拟实际生活的会话，尽管如此，这四五十分钟的一节课，对于学生来说都弥足珍贵。我们建议教师不要过多地使用PPT，您面对学生真诚坦然的微笑，亲切悦耳的话语，声情并茂的讲解与朗读，与学生面对面、心与心的交流，这是任何教材、任何课件都无法代替的。

口语课堂上，教师和学生都要动起来。再好的教材都是死的。语言是交际的工具，是最灵动、最活泼、最实用的。尤其是初级阶段，学生能不能尽快用汉语进行最实用的交际，对他们的影响巨大而深远。

口语应是带表情的动与说的结合。所以建议教师活用教材，把课堂当成“剧场”，把教材当成“剧本”，教师当好导演，学生当好演员，师生互动，把每节课都演成一幕话剧。

本教程分 4 册共 64 课，供零起点的汉语学习者使用 1 年。4 册书共出生词约 2000 个，多为常用词。

鉴于各个教学单位口语课的课时不统一，有多有少，所以，完全可以从本单位的实际出发，从教学对象的实际出发，灵活使用本教程。

编写体例

一、课文

本教程的课文多是情景会话。情景设计都基于来华留学生的学习和生活。编者的意图是，学习和练习这些会话，使学习者能熟练地运用它们，满足日常学习和生活的交际需要。

为了尽早培养学生的成段表达能力，本教程从第一册第10课起，就设置了一个“读后说”的练习项目。其内容都是一些小短文。

课文是重中之重！

课堂上教师要集中精力，用大量时间带领学生把课文读熟。教师要大声示范朗读，大声领读；同时，要求学生大声跟读、大声齐读、大声地单独朗读。

朗读是口语课堂教学和课外练习的主要方法。要鼓励学生大声地、反复地朗读，让学生通过朗读感受汉语的语音语调和语气，领略汉语的语言美。不论是会话课文还是叙述短文，都要求学生最少要朗读十遍以上，达到熟读成诵的程度。这样，也只有这样，用的时候才能脱口而出。

通过一年的训练，大多数学生的口语能力应能基本满足日常学习和生活的交际需要。这是被多年教学实践证明了的。

第一、二册（1～32课）的课文都配有汉语拼音，同时提供英文译文供学生参考。拼音是为了减少学生朗读的困难，英文译文是为了减少学生理解的困难。我们的教学对象大多具有高中以上学历，尽管英语不一定是每个学生的母语，但本教程的内容都是基础的日常会话，英文译文对他们理解课文应该有所帮助。

第三、四册（33～64课）除了生词加注拼音和英文释义外，课文不再加注拼音，也不再提供英文译文。

效果如何，要由教学实践来检验。我们希望听到一线教师的意见和建议，以便及时修正。

二、生词

本教程每课的生词部分都有拼音、词性和英文释义。

三、注释

口语课堂教学没有讲练语法的任务，因此，本教程的注释只是对课文中出现的一些语法点或重点词语的用法加以简要的说明，为教师教学提供一些方便。例句可供学习者参考。

四、练习

口语课重在培养学生“说”的言语技能，但听说读写这四项言语技能既相对独立又相互依存，既相互制约又相互促进。听不懂，一定不会说；读不懂，也一定影响说。没有大量的输入，就不可能有理想的输出。因此，口语课要达到预期的效果，必须充分利用各项言语技能的相互促进作用，通过有效的输入，激发表达欲望，促进齿舌运动，使学习者发出正确的汉语语音语调，说出正确的有交际意义的句子，从而达到日常学习和生活想要达到的交际目的。

本教程通用的练习是：朗读并分辨近音字词的语音语调、替换、选词填空、完成句子或会话并大声朗读、结合自身实际回答问题等。

口语课必须重视语音语调的训练。因此，本教程始终把语音语调的练习放在非常重要的位置。教材在这方面的努力，也是为教学做个提示：要想让学生说一口正确的汉语普通话，教师的作用是教材无法代替的。

练习要求学生课外完成，教师可及时检查和纠正，以提高学生的学习质量。

练习不仅是复练课堂所学，同时希望学生能够通过做练习，培养自学能力。严格地说，没有自学能力的学生不可能成才。在网络时代，只要想学、爱学，随时都可以学习。要引导学生刻苦自学、努力成才。所以，本教程在练习中一再提示，遇到不懂的词语、不懂的文化知识点，要去问百度、问谷歌，要随手去查电子词典——它们都是课外的“老师”。教师要鼓励学生自学，帮助学生培养良好的学习习惯。

在初级阶段，受词汇、语法的制约，会话课文都是情景会话。情景会话就必然受情景的限定。为了弥补初级口语会话的不足，我们在每课练习部分的最后，添加了一个“怎么表达”，这实际就是交际会话。一般说来，交际会话的句子和会话不太受情景的制约。需要说明的是，这也不属于课堂教学的内容，而是为学生自学准备的。

练习中的诗词和著名词句都是学生自学的内容。出诗词的目的是想利用其合辙押韵的特点，培养学生的朗读兴趣，同时也为他们今后的深造奠定基础。一些我们耳熟能详的词句，让学生接触一下，不无益处。

本教程的编写得到业内朋友的指导和帮助，北京语言大学出版社也给予大力支持，在此表示衷心的感谢。

编者

2022 年 6 月

Preface

Spoken Chinese Course is written for Chinese beginners. It is suitable for the academic institutions developing credential or non-credential education, as well as teaching Chinese for speakers of other languages.

The compiling idea of this course is to strive to cultivate students' talents.

The foreign students who choose to study Chinese, especially those who come to China to study Chinese, are at their best ages in life. They come all the way to China, to us, to pursue their dreams of life and learn Chinese with us, thus we can't let them down. We must hold the belief to cultivate students' talents. Even if they just study for a year or so, we should consider their future development.

The oral class is a single-skill training course.

While the listening and reading classes focus on input, the oral class stresses output. Therefore, students are required to speak as much as possible in class, and teachers are required to stimulate students' desire to express themselves adopting all kinds of teaching methods and techniques by the aid of the coursebook. Genuine conversations should take place between the teacher and students, as well as among students, in order to develop and train students' oral expression ability. After one year's study, students should be able to have daily communication in Chinese, and lay a solid foundation for their further study in higher grades or other majors (e.g. medicine, engineering, etc.).

The oral class should be a theater for the teacher to interact with students and demonstrate the coursebook.

We hope that the teacher can make full use of the class and the face-to-face context between him/her and students to guide and make teacher-student and student-student conversations. Classroom conversation is of course a conversation that stimulates real life. Nevertheless, the 40- to 50-minute lesson is especially valuable for students. We suggest teachers try not to use PPT too much. Your sincere and calm smile, kind and sweet words, remarkable explanation and reading aloud, and your face-to-face and heart-to-heart communication with students cannot be replaced by any coursebook or courseware.

In the oral Chinese class, both the teacher and students should be active. No matter how good the coursebook is, it is rigid. Language is the tool of communication. It is the most intelligent, active and practical. Especially in the primary stage, whether students can use Chinese to communicate as soon as possible has a huge and far-reaching impact on them.

Spoken language should be a combination of expressive movement and speech. So teachers are advised to make flexible use of the coursebook. Teachers should take the classroom as a theater and the coursebook as the playscript. The teacher should act as the director, while students should act as actors and actresses. They should interact with each other to put on a play in each class.

This course contains four books with 64 lessons. It is suitable for Chinese beginners and can be used for one year. There are about 2,000 new words in the four books, most of which are common words.

Since the hours for the oral class vary in each institution, you can use this coursebook flexibly according to the actual conditions of your institution and your students.

Compiling style:

I. Texts

The texts in this coursebook are mostly situation conversations. The situations are based on the study and life of foreign students in China. The compilers aim to make students learn and practice these conversations so as to use them proficiently and meet their communicative needs in study and life.

In order to develop students' ability to express themselves in paragraph as early as possible, a "speaking after reading" part is designed from Lesson 10 of Book 1. All the texts in this part are short essays.

Texts are the most important!

In class, the teacher should focus on texts and spend much time to lead students to read texts fluently. The teacher should model reading aloud and ask students to follow, and read aloud together and individually.

Reading aloud is the main method of oral classroom teaching and extracurricular practice. Encourage students to read aloud and repeatedly. Let students perceive the pronunciation, intonation and tones of Chinese and the beauty of Chinese by reading aloud.

Whether it is a conversation text or a narrative essay, the teacher should require students to read it aloud for at least ten times to reach the level of reciting it. In this way, and only in this way, can students blurt it out when using it.

Through one year's training, most students should be able to communicate in their daily study and life. This has been proved by years of teaching practice.

Pinyin and English translation for the texts are provided in Books 1 and 2 (Lessons 1-32). The Pinyin is added to make it easier for students to read the texts aloud, and the English translation is provided to reduce students' difficulty in understanding. Most of our students have a senior high school education or above. Although English is not necessarily every student's first language, all the content of this coursebook is basic and daily conversations, and the English translation should be helpful for them to understand the texts.

In Books 3 and 4 (Lessons 33-64), except for the Pinyin and English definition for the new words, no Pinyin and English translation for the texts are provided. The effect will be tested by the teaching practice. We hope to hear the opinions and suggestions from the teachers, so as to make timely revisions.

II. New Words

The Pinyin and English definition are provided for the new words in each lesson in the coursebook.

III. Notes

Grammar is not taught and practiced in the oral class. Therefore, the notes in this coursebook are only brief explanations of some grammatical points or key words and expressions that appear in the texts, to provide convenience for teaching. Example sentences are for students' reference.

IV. Exercises

Oral class focuses on developing students' speaking skills. However, the four language skills of listening, speaking, reading and writing are relatively independent on one hand, but dependent on each other on the other hand. If you don't understand what was said, you can't speak. If you don't understand what was written, your speaking skills will also be affected. Without a large amount of input, it is impossible to have ideal output. Therefore, to achieve the expected effect in oral class, we must make full use of the mutual promotion of various language skills. Through effective input, the desire to express is stimulated, and the tongue and teeth movements are promoted. Students are able to produce correct pronunciation and intonation of Chinese, and say the correct sentences with communicative meanings, so as to achieve the communicative purpose needed in daily study and life.

The common exercises in this coursebook include reading aloud and distinguishing the pronunciation and intonation of similar words, substitution, choosing words to fill in the blanks, completing the sentences or conversations and reading them aloud, and answering the questions according to the students' actual situations.

The training of pronunciation and intonation is very important in oral class. Therefore, this coursebook always attaches great importance to the pronunciation and intonation exercises. The effort of the coursebook in this regard is also a reminder for teaching: to make students speak Mandarin correctly, the role of teachers cannot be replaced by coursebooks.

Students are required to finish the exercises after class. Teachers can check and correct them in time to improve the quality of students' study.

The exercises are designed not only to practice what students have learned in class, but also to train students' self-study ability. Strictly speaking, students without self-study ability can't be successful. In the Internet age, as long as you want to and love to learn, you can learn at any time. Teachers should guide students to study hard independently and become successful. Therefore, the course in the exercises always suggests students to consult Baidu, Google, or electronic dictionaries when meeting unfamiliar words, expressions or cultural knowledge, for they are extracurricular "teachers". Teachers should encourage students to study by themselves and help them develop good study habits.

Restricted by vocabulary and grammar in the primary stage, all the conversational texts are situation conversations. In order to make up for the deficiency of primary oral conversations, we add a "how to express" part at the end of the exercises in each lesson. They are actually communicative conversations. Generally speaking, communicative sentences and conversations are less situational. It should be noted that this part is prepared for students to study on their own instead of being taught in class.

The well-known sayings in the exercises are for students to study on their own. The purpose is to guide students to perceive the rhymes in the poems so as to develop their interests in reading aloud and lay a foundation for their further study. It is useful for students to get an initial understanding of some poems and sentences we are familiar with.

We sincerely appreciate the guidance and help from friends in this field, as well as the strong support by Beijing Language and Culture University Press when compiling this coursebook.

Compilers

In June 2022

致学习者

亲爱的同学们：

当你拿起这本书，开始学习汉语口语的时候，你的人生便开始了新的旅程。

当你离开家乡，告别父母、兄弟、同学、朋友来到中国这个陌生国度的时候，你可能有诸多的不适应。

不过没关系。任何人初到异国他乡，都会有这种感觉的。

初来乍到，一句汉语也不会说，一个汉字也不认识，一个朋友都没有，你会感到孤单、寂寞，你会感到无助、痛苦。想家，想爸爸妈妈，想兄弟姐妹，想同学朋友，甚至会哭鼻子，恨不得马上飞回国去。

不过，你一定明白，眼前的这些困难都是暂时的，很快就会过去；过去了，你将由此踏上成才之路。

你要想到自己的未来，想到你是在学习人类最美的语言之一，也是当今世界历史最悠久、使用人数最多的语言之一——汉语！

汉语之美，美不胜收；汉字之妙，妙不可言。

要让自己冷静下来，想一想：今后的路该怎么走？

不必讳言，对于来自世界各国的学习者来说，汉语的确很难学。尽管书里说不难，但是老师心里明白，学好一种外语，对谁来说都不容易。

但"艰难困苦，玉汝于成"，"吃得苦中苦，才有甜上甜"。不经历风雨，难以见彩虹，没有人能随随便便地成功。希望你放平心态，放松心情，准备迎接各种挑战。为了你，为了你的家人，相信你一定不怕苦、不怕难，勇敢地闯过一道道难关，胜利到达成功的彼岸，实现自己美好的理想，成就自己理想的人生。

为此，根据我们几十年教外国留学生的经验，向同学们提出以下几点希望。

1. 无论如何，都应该坚持每天到教室上课

学得好的学生不一定是班上最聪明的学生，但一定是最努力的学生。希望同学们能天天和你的老师、同学见面，天天和他们一起度过这愉快美好的课堂时光。上课不仅仅是学汉语，更是为了培养自己高尚的人品和高贵的人格，使自己成为一个自律且优秀的人。

2．课后一定要认真做练习

学习外语，遇到不会、不懂的词语和句子是难免的。如今是网络时代，只要你想学，处处都能找到老师。所以我们一再强调：问百度、问谷歌、查电子词典。

要努力培养自己的自学能力。可以说，没有自学能力的人不可能成才。世界上凡是学有所成的人，都有非凡的自学能力。

老师领进门，修行在个人。

那些杰出的、优秀的人虽然都有老师，但他们最后都比自己的老师更优秀！也希望你们能踏着老师的肩膀，奋勇地攀登你们人生的高峰。

3. 要预习，预习比复习更重要

要变"要我学"为"我要学"，使自己时时处于主动的地位。

我们说预习比复习更重要，就是因为预习是你在主动地学。

学习外语，一定要走在老师的前边。现在的学习条件这么好，只要你有志气、肯努力，就要在上课前，把第二天要学的课文、生词都预习预习，一遍、两遍……，或者读一读、记一记。这样，你到教室去上课，将不会再有"难"的苦恼，而会觉得是一种美妙的享受。

4. 多和中国人交往

语言是交际的工具。到生活中去，到中国社会中去，社会生活永远有课堂上学不到的东西。要相信，人类的大多数都是善良的，中国人也一样。只要你不怕、不害羞，你就会明白，在家靠父母，出门靠朋友。多交朋友，一定是一件非常惬意的事。在中国人面前说汉语，不要怕说错。要多说，一次说错了，再说一次可能就说对了。要不了多久，你一定能说一口流利的汉语，你的生活也会开辟一片新的天地。

至于将来做什么，将来会怎么样，请你多读书，书会告诉你的。

这本书和教这本书的老师都是你的朋友，他们将陪伴你一路走去，走向你理想的未来。

最想说的是：我们爱你们，所以献上这本书！

编者

2021 年 6 月初稿

2022 年 6 月定稿

To Students

Dear students,

When you pick up this book and begin to learn spoken Chinese, your will start a new journey in your life.

When you leave your hometown, say goodbye to your parents, siblings, classmates and friends, and come to China—an unfamiliar country, you may feel much unadapted.

But it doesn't matter. Any new arrival to an alien place will have the same feeling.

When you first arrive in China, you cannot speak a word of Chinese, nor can you recognize any Chinese characters, or have any friends. You feel lonely, helpless and miserable. You miss your parents, siblings, classmates and friends. You even want to cry. You wish you would fly home immediately.

However, you must know that these immediate difficulties are temporary and will soon be overcome. When you overcome them, you will be on the road to success.

You have to think about your future, and that you are studying one of the most beautiful human languages, as well as one of the oldest and most spoken languages in the world today—Chinese!

The beauty of Chinese is too much to absorb. The wonder of Chinese characters is beyond expression.

You should calm yourself down and think about your road in future.

There is no denying the fact that Chinese is really difficult for students from all over the world. Although it is said in the books that Chinese is not difficult, teachers know that studying a foreign language well is not easy for anyone.

However, no pains, no gains. We hope that you will be prepared for challenges in a peaceful state of mind. For you and your family, we believe you won't be afraid of the difficulties and hardships, and you will get over the hurdles bravely before reaching the dreamland of success, realizing your goals, and achieving your ideal life.

To this end, based on our decades of experience in teaching foreign students, we hope you can do as follows:

1. Persist in attending class every day in any case

Those who do well in class are not necessarily the smartest students, but surely the most hard-working ones. We hope you can meet your teachers and classmates every day and spend the happy time with them in class. By attending class, you not only learn Chinese, but also cultivate noble character and make yourself a self-disciplined and excellent person.

2. Do exercises carefully after class

When studying a foreign language, it is inevitable to encounter words and sentences that you don't know or understand. In the Internet age, teachers can be found everywhere if you want to learn something. That's why we emphasize again and again that you should consult Baidu, Google, and electronic dictionaries.

Efforts should be made to develop your self-study ability. A person without the self study ability cannot be successful. Anyone in the world who is successful in learning has an extraordinary self-study ability.

The teacher may teach, but progress is up to the hard work of the individual.

Though those outstanding people have teachers, they become more excellent than their teachers in the end! We also hope that you can also stand on the shoulders of your teachers and climb the peak of your life bravely.

3. Pay attention to previewing, which is more important than reviewing

Change "make me study" to "I want to study", and take the initiative all the time. Previewing is more important than reviewing in that you are studying on your own initiative when you preview.

When you learn a foreign language, be sure to stay ahead of your teachers. Now the learning conditions are good. As long as you are ambitious and hardworking, you can preview, read and memorize the text and new words several times before class. In this way, when you go to class, you will feel wonderful rather than difficult.

4. Make more contact with Chinese people

Language is a tool of communication. You should experience Chinese life and society, where you can learn what you cannot learn in class. People are mostly kind, so are Chinese. As long as you are not afraid or shy, you will find that you need the support of friends when away from home. It is very pleasant to make more friends. Don't be afraid of making mistakes when speaking Chinese in front of Chinese people. Talk more. If you make a mistake at first, try again and you will probably be right. You will shortly be able to speak Chinese fluently. In addition, you will explore a new world in your life.

As to your future, read more books and you will find the answer.

Both this coursebook and the teacher who uses it in class are your friends, who will accompany you all the way to your ideal future.

What we want to say most is that we offer this book because we love you!

Compilers

First draft in June 2021

Final version in June 2022

一、汉语词类简称表

名称	简称	英文
1. 名词 míngcí	名	noun
2. 代词 dàicí	代	pronoun
3. 动词 dòngcí	动	verb
4. 助动词 zhùdòngcí	助动	auxiliary verb
5. 形容词 xíngróngcí	形	adjective
6. 数词 shùcí	数	numeral
7. 量词 liàngcí	量	measure word
8. 副词 fùcí	副	adverb
9. 介词 jiècí	介	preposition
10. 连词 liáncí	连	conjunction
11. 叹词 tàncí	叹	interjection
12. 拟声词 nǐshēngcí	拟声	onomatopoeia
13. 助词 zhùcí	助	particle
14. 词头 cítóu	头	prefix
15. 词尾 cíwěi	尾	suffix

二、汉语语法术语

1. 主语 zhǔyǔ subject
2. 谓语 wèiyǔ predicate
3. 宾语 bīnyǔ object
4. 定语 dìngyǔ attribute
5. 状语 zhuàngyǔ adverbial
6. 补语 bǔyǔ complement

（1）程度补语 chéngdù bǔyǔ degree complement

例如：形容词＋极了

这个电影好极了。

（2）状态补语 zhuàngtài bǔyǔ　　state complement

例如：动词＋得＋形容词 / 动词短语

他学得好不好？他学得很好。

他跑得快不快？他跑得不快。

你写得怎么样？我写得不太好。

他高兴得跳了起来。

（3）结果补语 jiéguǒ bǔyǔ　　result complement

例如：动词＋动词 / 形容词

我的作业做完了。

瓶子里的酒喝光了。

他把这本书翻译成了英语。

（4）趋向补语 qūxiàng bǔyǔ　　complement of direction

例如：动词＋来 / 去 / 上 / 下 / 进 / 出 / 回 / 过 / 起 / 上来 / 下去 / 回来 / 回去 / 过来 / 过去 / 起来 / 进来 / 进去……

他从楼上下来了。

我们从这儿上去吧。

我买回来一盆花。

他从外边里带进来一只小狗。

（5）可能补语 kěnéng bǔyǔ　　complement of potentiality

例如：动词＋得 / 不＋结果补语 / 趋向补语

中文报你看得懂看不懂？

我现在还听不懂中文广播。

屋子太小，坐不下二十个人。

你买得太多了，我吃不了。

沙发太大，搬不进去。

太重了，我提不动。

（6）数量补语 shùliàng bǔyǔ　　complement of quantity

例如：动词＋数量短语

他比我高五厘米。

姐姐比我大两岁。

（7）时量补语 shíliàng bǔyǔ complement of duration

例如：动词＋时量短语

我已经学了一年了。

他来了快一个月了。

（8）动量补语 dòngliàng bǔyǔ complement of frequency

例如：动词＋动量短语

我敲了一下门，但是没有人答应。

中国我已经来过两次了。

我把这篇文章从头到尾仔细看了一遍，没有发现错字。

香港我去过一回，台湾我还没有去过。

目 录 Contents

Dì-yī kè 第一课 Lesson 1

Ài 爱 Love

一 课文 Text

ài 爱	**Love**
Bàba māma ài wǒ. 爸爸妈妈爱我。	My father and mother love me.
Wǒ ài bàba māma. 我爱爸爸妈妈。	I love my father and mother.
Yéye nǎinai ài wǒ. 爷爷奶奶爱我。	My grandfather and grandmother love me.
Wǒ ài yéye nǎinai. 我爱爷爷奶奶。	I love my grandfather and grandmother.
Wǒ ài... 我爱……	I love...

二 生词 New Words

1	爱	ài	动	to love
2	爸爸	bàba	名	father
3	妈妈	māma	名	mother
4	我	wǒ	代	I; me
5	爷爷	yéye	名	grandfather
6	奶奶	nǎinai	名	grandmother

7 你	nǐ	代	you
8 好	hǎo	形	good; well; fine
9 大	dà	形	big; large
10 家	jiā	名	family; home
11 一	yī	数	one
12 五	wǔ	数	five
13 八	bā	数	eight

三 语音 Phonetics

1. 拼音 Pinyin

声母 Initials

b p m f d t n l

g k h j q x

韵母 Finals

a o e i u ü

ai ei ao ou an en ang eng

ia ie iao iu ian in iang ing

üe üan ün iong

ua uo uai ui uan un uang ueng ong

2. 拼音表 List of Pinyin

韵母	声母													
	b	p	m	f	d	t	n	l	g	k	h	j	q	x
a	ba	pa	ma	fa	da	ta	na	la	ga	ka	ha			
o	bo	po	mo	fo										
e			me		de	te	ne	le	ge	ke	he			

续表

韵母	声母													
	b	p	m	f	d	t	n	l	g	k	h	j	q	x
i	bi	pi	mi		di	ti	ni	li				ji	qi	xi
u	bu	pu	mu	fu	du	tu	nu	lu	gu	ku	hu			
ai	bai	pai	mai		dai	tai	nai	lai	gai	kai	hai			
ei	bei	pei	mei	fei	dei	tei	nei	lei	gei	kei	hei			
ao	bao	pao	mao		dao	tao	nao	lao	gao	kao	hao			
ou		pou	mou	fou	dou	tou	nou	lou	gou	kou	hou			
an	ban	pan	man	fan	dan	tan	nan	lan	gan	kan	han			
en	ben	pen	men	fen	den		nen		gen	ken	hen			
ang	bang	pang	mang	fang	dang	tang	nang	lang	gang	kang	hang			
eng	beng	peng	meng	feng	deng	teng	neng	leng	geng	keng	heng			
ia					dia			lia				jia	qia	xia
ie	bie	pie	mie		die	tie	nie	lie				jie	qie	xie
iao	biao	piao	miao		diao	tiao	niao	liao				jiao	qiao	xiao
iu			miu		diu		niu	liu				jiu	qiu	xiu
ian	bian	pian	mian		dian	tian	nian	lian				jian	qian	xian
in	bin	pin	min				nin	lin				jin	qin	xin
iang							niang	liang				jiang	qiang	xiang
ing	bing	ping	ming		ding	ting	ning	ling				jing	qing	xing
ü							nü	lü				ju	qu	xu
üe							nüe	lüe				jue	que	xue
üan												juan	quan	xuan
ün												jun	qun	xun
iong												jiong	qiong	xiong
ua									gua	kua	hua			
uo					duo	tuo	nuo	luo	guo	kuo	huo			

续表

韵母	声母													
	b	p	m	f	d	t	n	l	g	k	h	j	q	x
uai									guai	kuai	huai			
ui					dui	tui			gui	kui	hui			
uan					duan	tuan	nuan	luan	guan	kuan	huan			
un					dun	tun		lun	gun	kun	hun			
uang									guang	kuang	huang			
ueng														
ong					dong	tong	nong	long	gong	kong	hong			

四 注释 Notes

(一) 书写规则 Rules for writing syllables

以 i 开头的音节，i 要写成 y，如 ia—ya；以 u 开头的音节，u 要写成 w，如 ua—wa。i、u、ü 也可自成音节，自成音节时分别写成 yi、wu、yu。

If a syllable begins with i, i should be written as y, i.e., ia-ya; if a syllable begins with u, u should be written as w, i.e., ua-wa. i, u and ü may form syllables alone. They are written as yi, wu and yu respectively.

ia —— ya　　uo —— wo　　uai —— wai

ian —— yan　　uen —— wen　　uang —— wang

(二) 声调 Tones

汉语普通话有四个基本声调，声调符号分别是：ˉ（第一声）、ˊ（第二声）、ˇ（第三声）、ˋ（第四声）。

Mandarin Chinese has four basic tones. The marks of them are: ˉ (the 1st tone), ˊ (the 2nd tone), ˇ (the 3rd tone) and ˋ (the 4th tone).

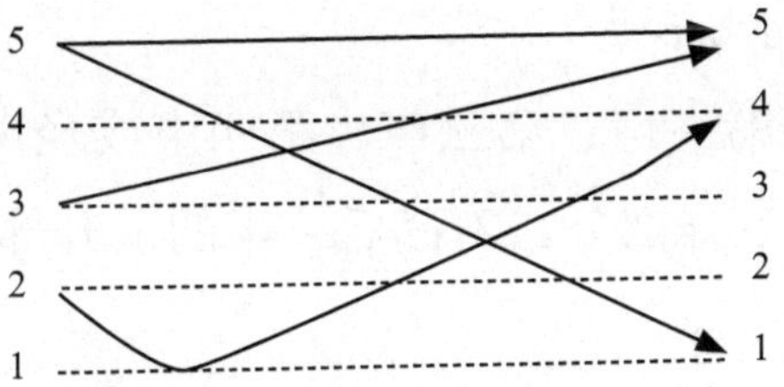

声调不同，表达的意义不同。例如：

Different tones may express different meanings, e.g.,

bā
八
eight

bá
拔
to pull

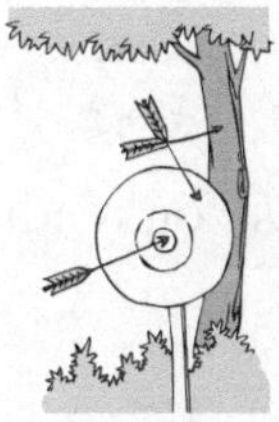

bǎ
靶
target

bà
爸
dad

bā	bá	bǎ	bà
eight	to pull	target	dad
mā	má	mǎ	mà
mom	numb	horse	to scold
yī	yí	yǐ	yì
one	to move	chair	a hundred million

（三）三声变调 The 3rd tone sandhi

1. 两个第三声音节连读时，前一个要读成第二声。例如：

When a 3rd tone is immediately followed by another 3rd tone, the former is pronounced as the 2nd tone, e.g.

ˇ + ˇ → ˊ + ˇ

nǐ hǎo → ní hǎo

hěn hǎo → hén hǎo

měihǎo → méihǎo

2. 半三声 The half 3rd tone

第三声音节后边跟第一声、第二声、第四声或轻声音节时，读作半三声，即只读第三声前一半的下降部分，不读后一半的上升部分，读完下降部分马上接读后面的音节。例如：

A 3rd-tone syllable is pronounced as a half 3rd tone when it is immediately followed by a 1st-, 2nd-, 4th- or neutral-tone syllable, which means only the first half (the falling part) of the tone is articulated and is immediately followed by the next syllable, e.g.,

hǎotīng	hǎodú	hǎokàn	hǎo ma
好听	好读	好看	好吗
pleasant to hear	easy on reading	good-looking	how are you

（四）轻声 The neutral tone

汉语中有些音节不带声调（不管它们所代表的汉字是第几声），念得很轻、很短，这样的音节叫轻声。轻声音高受前面一个音节声调的影响而有变化。例如：

Some syllables in Chinese are toneless (disregarding the tones of the characters they represent) and are pronounced light and short. These syllables are called neutralized tones or neutral tones. The pitch of a neutral tone is affected by the tone of the preceding syllable, e.g.

bàba	māma	yéye	nǎinai
gēge	mèimei	nǐmen	hǎo ma

注意：在拼写中，轻声音节无调号。

Note: In transcription, a neutral tone does not carry any tone mark.

五 练习 Exercises

（一）唱四声 Practice the tones

āi	ái	ǎi	ài	——	ài	爱
wō		wǒ	wò	——	wǒ	我

bā	bá	bǎ	bà	——	bà	爸
mā	má	mǎ	mà	——	mā	妈
yē	yé	yě	yè	——	yé	爷
		nǎi	nài	——	nǎi	奶
nī	ní	nǐ	nì	——	nǐ	你
hāo	háo	hǎo	hào	——	hǎo	好
dā	dá	dǎ	dà	——	dà	大
jiā	jiá	jiǎ	jià	——	jiā	家
yī	yí	yǐ	yì	——	yī	一
wū	wú	wǔ	wù	——	wǔ	五
bā	bá	bǎ	bà	——	bā	八

（二）**朗读下列带三声的词语，注意三声变调** Read aloud the following words and expressions with the 3rd tones and pay attention to the 3rd tone sandhi

1. 三声 + 三声 The 3rd tone + the 3rd tone

nǐ hǎo 你 好	hěn hǎo 很 好	měihǎo 美好
wǔbǎi 五百	gěi nǐ 给你	kěyǐ 可以

2. 半三声 The half 3rd tone

hǎotīng 好听	hǎodú 好读	hǎokàn 好看	hǎo ma 好 吗
nǐ hē 你喝	nǐ lái 你来	nǐ kàn 你看	nǐ de 你 的
qǐng tīng 请 听	nǐ máng 你 忙	wǒ qù 我去	nǐ ne 你呢
hěn gāo 很 高	hěn hóng 很 红	hěn màn 很 慢	hǎo ba 好 吧
yǔyīn 语音	yǔyán 语言	hěn nán 很 难	xǐhuan 喜欢

（三）朗读下列带轻声的词语 Read aloud the following words and expressions with the neutral tones

bàba	māma	yéye	nǎinai
gēge	mèimei	jiějie	dìdi
nǐmen	hǎo ma	bǎo le	pǎo le
bái de	hēi de	hóng de	lán de
hē ma	hē ba	mǎi ma	mǎi ba
qù ma	qù ba	lái ma	lái ba
duì ma	duì le	dǒng ma	dǒng le
lèi ma	lèi le	hǎo de	lǎo de

（四）怎么表达 How to express

Dǎ zhāohu, dào qiàn hé gǎnxiè
打招呼、道歉和感谢 greeting, apology & thanks

Nǐ hǎo!
1. A：你好！
Hello!

Nǐ hǎo!
B：你好！
Hello!

Duìbuqǐ!
2. A：对不起！
Sorry!

Méi guānxi!
B：没关系！
Never mind / It doesn't matter / That's all right.

Xièxie nǐ!
3. A：谢谢你！
Thank you!

Bú kèqi!

B：不客气！

You're welcome!

（五）**请和同学表演以上会话** Please act out the above conversations with your classmates

（六）**请欣赏下列著名的词句** Please enjoy the following well-known saying

Rénzhě ài rén.

仁者爱人。

The benevolent love others.

提示：如果不懂，就查百度、谷歌或电子词典。

Prompt: If you don't understand, please consult Baidu, Google or an electronic dictionary.

Dì-èr kè

第二课 Lesson 2

Xué Hànyǔ, xíng tiānxià

学汉语，行天下

Learn Chinese, and travel all over China

一 课文 Text

Xué Hànyǔ, xíng tiānxià
学汉语，行天下

Nǐ xuéxí Hànyǔ?
A：你学习汉语？
Duì!
B：对！
Hǎo! Xuéhǎo Hànyǔ, néng xíng tiānxià.
A：好！学好汉语，能行天下。

Learn Chinese, and travel all over China

A: Do you learn Chinese?

B: Yes!

A: Good! If you learn Chinese well, you can travel all over China.

二 生词 New Words

1	学	xué	动	to study; to learn
2	汉语	Hànyǔ	名	Chinese (language)
3	行	xíng	动	to go; to travel
4	天下	tiānxià	名	the whole country or the world
5	学习	xuéxí	动	to study; to learn
6	对	duì	形	right; correct
7	能	néng	助动	can; to be able to

三 语音 Phonetics

1. 拼音 Pinyin

声母 Initials

d t n l
g k h
z c s

韵母 Finals

i [ɿ] a e ei ao ou an en
ang eng ong
u uo uei (ui) uan uen (un)
uang ueng ü üe üan ün

2. 拼音表 List of Pinyin

韵母	声母									
	d	t	n	l	g	k	h	z	c	s
i [ɿ]								zi	ci	si
a	da	ta	na	la	ga	ka	ha	za	ca	sa
e	de	te	ne	le	ge	ke	he	ze	ce	se
ei	dei	tei	nei	lei	gei	kei	hei	zei	cei	
ao	dao	tao	nao	lao	gao	kao	hao	zao	cao	sao
ou	dou	tou	nou	lou	gou	kou	hou	zou	cou	sou
an	dan	tan	nan	lan	gan	kan	han	zan	can	san
en	den		nen		gen	ken	hen	zen	cen	sen
ang	dang	tang	nang	lang	gang	kang	hang	zang	cang	sang
eng	deng	teng	neng	leng	geng	keng	heng	zeng	ceng	seng
ong	dong	tong	nong	long	gong	kong	hong	zong	cong	song
u	du	tu	nu	lu	gu	ku	hu	zu	cu	su

续表

韵母	声母									
	d	t	n	l	g	k	h	z	c	s
uo	duo	tuo	nuo	luo	guo	kuo	huo	zuo	cuo	suo
uei (ui)	dui	tui			gui	kui	hui	zui	cui	sui
uan	duan	tuan	nuan	luan	guan	kuan	huan	zuan	cuan	suan
uen (un)	dun	tun		lun	gun	kun	hun	zun	cun	sun
uang					guang	kuang	huang			
ueng										
ü			nü	lü						
üe			nüe	lüe						
üan										
ün										

四 注释 Notes

（一）韵母 -i [ʅ] The final -i [ʅ]

zi、ci、si 的韵母是舌尖前音 [ʅ]，用字母 -i 表示。因为汉语普通话中 [i] 不出现在 z、c、s 之后，所以 zi、ci、si 中的韵母 i 一定不能读成 [i]。

The finals in zi, ci and si are the dental [ʅ]. It is represented by the letter -i. Since [i] never appears immediately after z, c or s in Mandarin Chinese, the final i cannot be pronounced as [i].

（二）书写规则 Rules for writing syllables

1. 以 ü 开头的音节，音节开头要加上 y，ü 上面的两点要去掉。

If a syllable begins with ü, y should be added at the beginning, and the two dots on the top of ü should be omitted.

ü——yu　　üe —— yue　　üan —— yuan　　ün —— yun

2. ü、üe、üan、ün 和 j、q、x 相拼时，ü 上面的两点要去掉，写成：ju、jue、juan、jun。

When ü, üe, üan and ün are combined with j, q and x, the two dots on the top of ü should be omitted. The syllables are written as ju, jue, juan and jun, etc.

qu	que	quan	qun
xu	xue	xuan	xun

3. ü 与 n、l 相拼时，仍写成 ü。例如：nǚ、lǚ。

When ü is combined with n or l, it is still written as ü, e.g., nǚ, lǚ.

4. iou 前面加声母时要写成 iu，例如：liù。

When iou is combined with an initial, it should be written as iu, e.g., liù.

五 练习 Exercises

（一）唱四声 Practice the four tones

xuē	xué	xuě	xuè	——	xué	学
xī	xí	xǐ	xì	——	xí	习
hān	hán	hǎn	hàn	——	hàn	汉
yū	yú	yǔ	yù	——	yǔ	语
hāo	háo	hǎo	hào	——	hǎo	好
xīng	xíng	xǐng	xìng	——	xíng	行
tiān	tián	tiǎn		——	tiān	天
xiā	xiá		xià	——	xià	下

（二）辨音辨调 Distinguish the pronunciations and tones

zá	cā	sā	zé	cè	sè
zì	cí	sì	zú	cū	sū

zǎn	cān	sān	zāng	cāng	sāng
zěn	cēn	sēn	zēng	céng	sēng

zìdiǎn	cídiǎn	cíyì	cíxù
zàijiàn	zàixiàn	xiànzài	gāngcái
zànxǔ	zànyù	diǎn zàn	sǎnmàn
zāogāo	zǎocāo	zàojiǎ	zàojià
zǒngshì	cóngshì	zuìhòu	suíhòu
zuǒyòu	suǒyǒu	zuòwén	suǒ mén
cōngmíng	cōngmǐn	cóngqián	cóngyán
sì diǎn	sì tiān	cǎisè	cāicè
sǎochú	zǎo chū	dǎsǎo	zácǎo
bǐsài	cúnzài	cūnzi	sūnzi
zǔguó	cùjìn	sùdù	dìtú

（三）**请欣赏下列著名的词句** Please enjoy the following well-known saying

Shàozhuàng bù nǔlì, lǎodà tú shāngbēi.

少壮 不努力，老大 徒 伤悲。

Laziness in youth spells regret in old age.

Dì-sān kè 第三课 Lesson 3
Zhēn shàn měi, hé wéi guì 真善美，和为贵
Pursue truth, goodness and beauty; peace is most precious

一 课文 Text

Zhēn shàn měi, hé wéi guì
真善美，和为贵

Xuéshēng: Lǎoshī, rénshēng zěnyàng cái xìngfú?
学生：老师，人生 怎样 才 幸福？

Lǎoshī: Zhuīqiú zhēn, shàn, měi!
老师：追求 真、善、美！

Xuéshēng: Shìjiè yīnggāi zěnmeyàng?
学生：世界 应该 怎么样？

Lǎoshī: Shìjiè yào hépíng, hé wéi guì!
老师：世界要和平，和为贵！

Pursue truth, goodness and beauty; peace is most precious

Student: Madam, how can we live a happy life?

Teacher: Pursue truth, goodness and beauty!

Student: What should the world be like?

Teacher: The world needs peace, and peace is most precious.

二 生词 New Words

1	真	zhēn	形	true; real; genuine
2	善	shàn	形	kind-hearted; good; virtuous
3	美	měi	形	beautiful
4	和	hé	形	harmonious; peaceful; kind; gentle

5	为	wéi	动	to be; to mean; to act as
6	贵	guì	形	valuable; precious
7	学生	xuéshēng	名	student
8	老师	lǎoshī	名	teacher
9	人生	rénshēng	名	life
10	怎样	zěnyàng	代	how
11	才	cái	副	not...until; then and only then; only when
12	幸福	xìngfú	形	happy
13	追求	zhuīqiú	动	to seek; to pursue; to go after
14	世界	shìjiè	名	world
15	应该	yīnggāi	助动	should; ought to
16	怎么样	zěnmeyàng	代	how about
17	要	yào	动	to need
18	和平	hépíng	名	peace

三 语音 Phonetics

1. 拼音 Pinyin

声母 Initials

zh ch sh r

韵母 Finals

a e i [ʅ] ai ei ao ou an en
ang eng ong
u ua uo uai uei (ui) uan uen (un) uang

2. 拼音表 List of Pinyin

韵母	声母			
	zh	ch	sh	r
a	zha	cha	sha	
e	zhe	che	she	re
i [ʅ]	zhi	chi	shi	ri
ai	zhai	chai	shai	
ei	zhei		shei	
ao	zhao	chao	shao	rao
ou	zhou	chou	shou	rou
an	zhan	chan	shan	ran
en	zhen	chen	shen	ren
ang	zhang	chang	shang	rang
eng	zheng	cheng	sheng	reng
ong	zhong	chong		rong
u	zhu	chu	shu	ru
ua	zhua	chua	shua	rua
uo	zhuo	chuo	shuo	ruo
uai	zhuai	chuai	shuai	
uei (ui)	zhui	chui	shui	rui
uan	zhuan	chuan	shuan	ruan
uen (un)	zhun	chun	shun	run
uang	zhuang	chuang	shuang	

四 注释 Notes

韵母 -i [ʅ] The final -i [ʅ]

zhi、chi、shi、ri 中的韵母是舌尖后音 [ʅ]，用字母 -i 表示。因为汉语普通

话中 [i] 不出现在 zh、ch、sh、r 之后，所以 zhi、chi、shi、ri 中的韵母 i 一定不能读成 [i]。

The finals in zhi, chi, shi and ri are the blade-palatal [ʅ]. It is represented by the letter -i. Since [i] never appears immediately after zh, ch, sh or r in Mandarin Chinese, the final i in zhi, chi, shi and ri cannot be pronounced as [i].

五 练习 Exercises

（一）唱四声 Practice the four tones

	rén	rěn	rèn	——	rén	人
shēng	shéng	shěng	shèng	——	shēng	生
xīng	xíng	xǐng	xìng	——	xìng	幸
fū	fú	fǔ	fù	——	fú	福
zhuī			zhuì	——	zhuī	追
qiū	qiú	qiǔ		——	qiú	求
zhēn		zhěn	zhèn	——	zhēn	真
shān		shǎn	shàn	——	shàn	善
	méi	měi	mèi	——	měi	美
shī	shí	shǐ	shì	——	shì	世
jiē	jié	jiě	jiè	——	jiè	界
yāo	yáo	yǎo	yào	——	yào	要
hē	hé		hè	——	hé	和
pīng	píng			——	píng	平
wēi	wéi	wěi	wèi	——	wéi	为
guī		guǐ	guì	——	guì	贵

（二）辨音辨调 Distinguish the pronunciations and tones

zhī	chī	shì	rì
zhè	chē	shè	rè

zhàn	chǎn	shān	rán
zhāng	cháng	shàng	ràng
zhēn	chèn	shén	rén
zhèng	chéng	shēng	réng

zá	zhá	cā	chá	sǎ	shǎ
zé	zhé	cè	chè	sè	shè
zì	zhì	cí	chí	sì	shì

sìshí	shísì	xiūxi	xiāoxi
zhīdào	chídào	chūntiān	shùnjiān
chūn nuǎn	chūnwǎn	zhēnchéng	zhēnzhèng
Chángchéng	chángzhēng	qīwàng	xīwàng
Zhōngwén	chōngfèn	chēzhàn	shāngdiàn
chéngnián	qīngnián	chuán shang	chuáng shang
zhījǐ	shíjī	shènglì	jīnglì
shēnghuó	jīngguò	shòushāng	shāngxīn
rènshi	rénshì	línshí	línshī
rénlèi	rénwéi	rìlì	rìjì

（三）朗读下列带三声的词语，注意三声变调 Read aloud the following words and expressions with the 3rd tones and pay attention to the tone sandhi

jiǎndān	hǎi biān	hǎixiān	hǎochī
biǎoyáng	gǎnjué	jiǎnchá	lǚxíng
yǔfǎ	měihǎo	biǎoyǎn	kěyǐ
bǐsài	děngdài	biǎoshì	gǎnxiè

（四）朗读下列带轻声的词语 Read aloud the following words with the neutral tones

kuàizi 筷子	sháozi 勺子	chāzi 叉子	dāozi 刀子
zhuōzi 桌子	yǐzi 椅子	píngzi 瓶子	qǐzi 起子

（五）朗读下列词语 Read aloud the following phrases

zhēnrén 真人	zhēn shì 真事	rén zhēn 人真	qíng zhēn 情真
shàn rén 善人	shànxīn 善心	rén shàn 人善	xīn shàn 心善
rén měi 人美	xīn měi 心美	shān měi 山美	shuǐ měi 水美
hépíng 和平	héxié 和谐	hémù 和睦	héshàn 和善

（六）根据课文回答下列问题 Answer the questions

A：人生怎样才幸福？

B：______________________________。

A：世界应该怎么样呢？

B：______________________________。

（七）请欣赏下列著名的词句 Please enjoy the following famous phrases

Jūnzǐ hé ér bù tóng.
君子和而不同。

Gentlemen seek harmony but does not necessarily agree with others.

Dì-sì kè

第四课 Lesson 4

Bàba māma, nǐmen hǎo ma

爸爸妈妈，你们好吗 Mom and Dad, how are you

一 课文 Text

Bàba māma, nǐmen hǎo ma

爸爸 妈妈，你们 好 吗

（玛丽跟爸爸妈妈通过视频互相问候）

Mǎlì: Bàba māma, nǐmen hǎo ma?
玛丽：爸爸妈妈，你们 好 吗？

Māma: Wǒmen hěn hǎo. Nǐ hǎo ma, Mǎlì?
妈妈：我们 很 好。你好 吗，玛丽？

Mǎlì: Wǒ yě hěn hǎo. Gēge hǎo ma?
玛丽：我 也很 好。哥哥 好 吗？

Māma: Nǐ gēge yě hěn hǎo.
妈妈：你哥哥也很 好。

Mǎlì: Mèimei zěnmeyàng?
玛丽：妹妹 怎么样？

Māma: Tā yě hěn hǎo.
妈妈：她 也 很 好。

Mǎlì: Gǒugou hǎo ma?
玛丽：狗狗 好 吗？

Bàba: Tā yě hěn hǎo! Hāha, wǒmen dōu hěn hǎo.
爸爸：它 也 很 好！哈哈，我们 都 很 好。

Mom and dad, how are you

(Mary is having a video chat with her parents.)

Mary: Mom and Dad, how are you?

Mom: We're fine. How are you, Mary?

Mary: I'm fine, too. How's my brother?

Mom: Your brother is fine, too.

Mary: How's my sister?

Mom: She is also very well.

Mary: How's the dog?

Dad: It is very well, too! Haha, we are all fine.

二 生词 New Words

1	你们	nǐmen	代	you (plural)
	们	men	后缀	*used after a personal pronoun or a noun to show plural number*
2	吗	ma	助	*used at the end of an interrogative sentence*
3	跟	gēn	介、动	with; to follow
4	通过	tōngguò	介	by means of; via
5	视频	shìpín	名	video
6	互相	hùxiāng	副	each other
7	问候	wènhòu	动	to ask after
8	我们	wǒmen	代	we; us
9	很	hěn	副	very
10	也	yě	副	too; also
11	哥哥	gēge	名	elder brother
	弟弟	dìdi	名	younger brother
12	妹妹	mèimei	名	younger sister
	姐姐	jiějie	名	elder sister
13	她	tā	代	she; her
	他	tā	代	he; him

14 狗	gǒu	名	dog
15 它	tā	代	it
16 哈	hā	拟声	ha; ha-ha (*sound of laughing with the mouth wide open, usu. reduplicated*)
17 都	dōu	副	all; both

专名 Zhuānmíng Proper Noun

玛丽	Mǎlì	Mary

三 注释 Notes

怎么问（1）：……吗？ Interrogation (1): Yes/No questions with "……吗？"

在陈述句句尾加上表示疑问的语气助词"吗"，构成汉语的是非问句。例如：

A yes/no question is formed by adding the interrogative modal particle "吗" to the end of a declarative sentence, e.g.,

1. A：爸爸妈妈，你们好吗？
   B：我们很好。
2. A：你好吗，玛丽？
   B：我也很好。

四 练习 Exercises

（一）朗读 Read aloud

1. 朗读下列带轻声的词语 Read aloud the following words and expressions with the neutral tones

wǒmen	nǐmen	tāmen		
bóbo	shūshu	gūgu	lǎolao	lǎoye

zhème	nàme	zěnme	shénme
máng ma	lèi ma	kě ma	è ma
zuò ba	chī ba	hē ba	shuō ba
xiǎng jiā le	xiǎng mā le	kū le ma	
xiàoxiao ba	tiàotiao ba		
chībǎo le	hēhǎo le	bù xiǎng le	

2. 朗读下列带三声的词语，注意三声变调 Read aloud the following words and expressions with the 3rd tones and pay attention to the tone sandhi

（1）三声＋三声 The 3rd tone + the 3rd tone

yǒuhǎo 友好	bǎodǎo 宝岛	bǎomǎn 饱满	bǎihǎo 摆好
bǎoguǎn 保管	bǎoxiǎn 保险	bǎoyǎng 保养	bǎonuǎn 保暖

（2）半三声 The half 3rd tone

bǎo le 饱 了	pǎo le 跑 了	hǎo le 好 了	shǎo le 少 了
lǎoshī 老师	lǎorén 老人	lǎoshì 老是	lǎoshi 老实
měi tiān 每 天	měi nián 每 年	měihuà 美化	měilì 美丽
hěn suān 很 酸	hěn tián 很 甜	hěn là 很 辣	hěn xián 很 咸

3. 朗读下列发音相近的词语 Read aloud the following words and expressions with similar pronunciations

bàba 爸爸	pà ma 怕吗	māma 妈妈	mà ma 骂 吗
wǒmen 我们	wǒ wèn 我 问	gēge 哥哥	gègè 个个
mèimei 妹妹	měiměi 每每	hěn hǎo 很 好	hěn shǎo 很 少
hěn è 很 饿	hěn kě 很 渴	hěn hóng 很 红	hěn píng 很 平

（二）**选词填空并朗读下列句子** Choose the appropriate words to fill in the blanks and read aloud the following sentences

1. 很　吗　呢　也　他

A：妈妈，你好________？

B：我________好。玛丽，你________？

A：我________很好。爸爸好________？

B：________也很好。

2. 它　好　都　她

A：我妹妹________吗？

B：________很好。

A：狗狗呢？

B：________也很好。我们________很好。

（三）**完成下列会话并大声朗读** Complete the following conversations and read them aloud

A：________________________________？

Hěn hǎo. Nǐ hǎo ma, Mǎlì?

B：很好。你好吗，玛丽？

Wǒ hěn hǎo. Gēge hǎo ma?

A：我很好。哥哥好吗？

B：________________________________。

Mèimei zěnmeyàng?

A：妹妹怎么样？

B：________________________________。

Gǒugou hǎo ma?

A：狗狗好吗？

B：________________________________。

（四）将 A、B 两列连线，组成正确的对话 Match A with B to make up appropriate dialogues

A	B
Nǐ hǎo! 你好！	Bú kèqi. 不客气。
Nǐ hǎo ma? 你好吗？	Méi guānxi. 没关系。
Nǐ máng ma? 你忙吗？	Zàijiàn! 再见！
Xièxie nǐ! 谢谢你！	Nǐ hǎo! 你好！
Duìbuqǐ! 对不起！	Wǒ bù máng. 我不忙。
Zàijiàn! 再见！	Wǒ hěn hǎo! 我很好！

（五）根据课文回答下列问题 Answer the following questions according to the text

1. 请说说玛丽家有几口人。
2. 她家都有什么人？

（六）和同学一起表演课文 Act out the text with your classmates

（七）怎么表达 How to express

dǎting
打听 asking about; inquiring

Wǒ xiàng nín dǎting yí gè rén. Nín rènshi Wáng jiàoshòu ma?
1. 我向您打听一个人。您认识王教授吗？
Excuse me. May I ask you about a person? Do you know Professor Wang?

Xǐshǒujiān zài nǎr?
2. A：洗手间在哪儿？
Where is the toilet?

Zǒuláng jìntóu yǒu yí gè.
B：走廊尽头有一个。
There is one at the end of the corridor.

（八）朗读中国经典诗词，请注意语音语调 Read aloud the classic Chinese poem and pay attention to the pronunciation and intonation

Jìng Yè Sī
静夜思

[Táng] Lǐ Bái
[唐] 李 白（701—762）

Chuáng qián míng yuè guāng, yí shì dìshang shuāng.
床 前 明 月 光，疑是 地上 霜。

Jǔ tóu wàng míng yuè, dī tóu sī gùxiāng.
举头 望 明 月，低 头 思 故乡。

（九）请欣赏下列著名的词句 Please enjoy the following well-known saying

Wànshì kāitóu nán.
万事 开头 难。

It is the first step that costs.

Dì-wǔ kè
第五课
Lesson 5

Nǐ jīntiān yǒu jǐ jié kè
你今天有几节课
How many classes do you have today

一 课文 Text

（一）你今天有几节课

Nǐ qù gōngyuán ma?
A：你 去 公园 吗？

Bú qù, wǒ qù xuéxiào, wǒ jīntiān yǒu kè.
B：不去，我 去 学校，我 今天 有 课。

Nǐ jīntiān yǒu jǐ jié kè?
A：你 今天 有 几节 课？

Yǒu liù jié kè.
B：有 六节课。

Nǐ yì xīngqī yǒu duōshao jié kè?
A：你一星期 有 多少 节课？

Yǒu èrshí duō jié kè ne.
B：有 二十 多 节 课 呢。

How many classes do you have today

A: Are you going to the park?

B: No, I am going to school. I have classes today.

A: How many classes do you have today?

B: Six.

A: How many classes do you have a week?

B: More than twenty.

（二）去公园

Wǒ qù gōngyuán, nǐ qù bu qù?
A：我 去 公园，你 去不去？

Qù.
B：去。

Wǒmen yìqǐ qù, hǎo ma?
A：我们一起去，好吗？

Hǎo a!
B：好啊！

Go to the park

A: I'm going to the park. Are you going there?

B: Yes, I am.

A: Shall we go together?

B: All right!

二 生词 New Words

1	今天	jīntiān	名	today
2	有	yǒu	动	to have
3	几	jǐ	代	how many
4	节	jié	量	*a measure word for lessons*
5	课	kè	名	lesson; course
6	去	qù	动	to go; to leave
7	公园	gōngyuán	名	park
8	不	bù	副	no
9	学校	xuéxiào	名	school
10	六	liù	数	six
	二	èr	数	two
	三	sān	数	three
	四	sì	数	four
	七	qī	数	seven
	九	jiǔ	数	nine

十	shí	数	ten
11 星期	xīngqī	名	week
12 多少	duōshao	代	how many; how much
13 多	duō	数、形	(*used after numerals*) more than; many; much
14 呢	ne	助	*used at the end of a declarative sentence to reinforce the assertion or play up the effect of exaggeration*
15 一起	yìqǐ	副	together
16 啊	a	助	*used at the end of a sentence to express agreement, defensiveness, urge, etc.*

三 注释 Notes

(一)"不"的变调 The tone sandhi of "不"

"不"的本调是第四声，但在另一个第四声音节前边时，变为第二声。例如：

The original tone of "不" is the 4th tone. If followed by a 4th-tone syllable, it is pronounced in the 2nd tone, e.g.,

bù hē	bù nán	bù hǎo	bú qù
bù gāo	bù lái	bù xiǎo	bú xiè

(二)"一"的变调 The tone sandhi of "一"

数词"一"的本调是第一声，在单独念、数数或读号码时，读本调。

The original tone of the numeral "一" is the 1st tone. When it is read alone or in counting or calling out numbers, its original tone is used.

"一"的发音根据后面音节的声调而变化。"一"后面的音节是第一、二、三声时，"一"读成第四声；"一"后面的音节是第四声时，"一"读成第二声。例如：

The tone of "一" may vary with the tone of the syllable that comes after it. If followed by a 1st-, 2nd- or 3rd-tone syllable, "一" is pronounced in the 4th tone; if followed by a 4th-tone syllable, it is pronounced in the 2nd tone, e.g.,

yì tiān	yì jié	yì bǎ	yíqiè
yìbān	yì yuán	yì běn	yí kè
yì jīn	yì nián	yìdiǎnr	yí jiàn

四 练习 Exercises

(一) 请读出下列数字 Please read out the following numbers

1	2	3	4	5	6	7	8	9	10
一	二	三	四	五	六	七	八	九	十
11	12	13	14	15	16	17	18	19	20
21	22	23	24	25	26	27	28	29	30

(二) 朗读 Read aloud

1. 朗读下列词语，注意"不"的变调 Read aloud the following words and expressions and pay attention to the tone sandhi of "不"

bù'ān	bùxíng	bù jiǎng	bú huì
bù shuō	bù nán	bù yǎn	bú kàn
bù suān	bù tián	bù mǎi	bú guì
bù huāng	bù máng	bù zǒu	bú lèi

bù kū 不哭	bù nán 不难	bù kǔ 不苦	bú là 不辣
pà ma 怕吗	bú pà 不怕	máng ma 忙吗	bù máng 不忙
kùn ma 困吗	bú kùn 不困	dǒng ma 懂吗	bù dǒng 不懂
bù zhī 不知	bùjué 不觉	bújiàn 不见	bú sàn 不散

2. 朗读下列词语，注意"一"的变调 Read aloud the following words and expressions and pay attention to the tone sandhi of "一"

yìbān	yì rén	yì běn	yí piàn
yì zhāng	yì céng	yì kǒu	yí gè
yì shuāng	yì huí	yì shǒu	yí jiàn
yì tiān	yì nián	yì bǐ	yídàn

3. 朗读下列发音相近的词语 Read aloud the following words and expressions with similar pronunciation

jīntiān 今天	míngtiān 明天	jīnnián 今年	míngnián 明年
zuótiān 昨天	zuò fàn 做饭	yǒu kè 有课	yóukè 游客
jǐ jié 几节	jìjié 季节	lǐbian 里边	wàibian 外边
gōngyuán 公园	gōngyǎn 公演	bú qù 不去	wǔqǔ 舞曲
yìqǐ 一起	yìqí 一齐	yìbān 一般	yíbàn 一半

（三）选词填空并朗读下列句子 Choose the appropriate words to fill in the blanks and read aloud the following sentences

多少　有　吗　节　不

A：你去公园________？
B：________去，我去学校，我今天有课。
A：你今天________几节课？
B：有六________课。
A：你一星期有________节课？
B：有二十多________课呢。

（四）完成下列会话并大声朗读 Complete the following conversations and read them aloud

A：你去公园吗？

B：________，我去学校，________________。

A：你今天有几节课？

B：________________。

A：你一星期有多少节课？

B：________________。

（五）和同学一起表演课文 Act out the text with your classmates

（六）怎么表达 How to express

ānwèi
安慰 comforting

Mànmàn lái, bié zháo jí.
1. 慢慢 来，别 着 急。
Take your time.

Tīng bu dǒng méi guānxi, mànmàn lái.
2. 听 不 懂 没 关系，慢慢 来。
It doesn't matter if you don't understand. Take your time.

Qiānwàn bié nánguò.
3. 千万 别 难过。
Never feel bad.

（七）朗读中国经典诗词，请注意语音语调 Read aloud the classic Chinese poem and pay attention to the pronunciation and intonation

Xiāngsī
相思

[Táng] Wáng Wéi
[唐]　王　维（701—761）

Hóngdòu shēng nánguó, chūn lái fā jǐ zhī.
红豆　生　南国，春　来 发 几 枝。
Yuàn jūn duō cǎixié,　cǐ wù zuì xiāngsī.
愿 君 多 采撷，此 物 最 相思。

（八）请欣赏下列著名的词句 Please enjoy the following well-known saying

Shìshang wú nánshì,　zhǐ pà yǒuxīnrén.
世上 无 难事，只 怕 有心人。
Nothing is impossible to a willing heart.

Dì-liù kè
第六课 Lesson 6

Nǐ xiǎng chī diǎnr shénme
你想吃点儿什么 What would you like to eat

一 课文 Text

（一）你想吃点儿什么

Nǐ è ma?
A：你饿吗？

Yǒudiǎnr è.
B：有点儿饿。

Nǐ xiǎng chī (yì)diǎnr shénme?
A：你想吃（一）点儿什么？

Zhèxiē shì shénme?
B：这些是什么？

Zhèxiē shì jiǎozi.
A：这些是饺子。

Nàxiē shì shénme?
B：那些是什么？

Nàxiē shì bāozi.
A：那些是包子。

Hǎochī ma?
B：好吃吗？

Mǎi yìxiē chángchang ba.
A：买一些尝尝吧。

À, zhēn hǎochī.
B：啊，真好吃。

What would you like to eat

A: Are you hungry?

B: Yes, a little.

A: What would you like to eat?

B: What are these?

A: They are dumplings.

B: What are those?

A: They are steamed stuffed buns.

B: Do they taste good?

A: Let's buy some to try.

B: Oh, it's yummy.

（二）这是什么茶

Zhè shì shénme?
A：这是什么？

Zhè shì chá.
B：这是茶。

Zhè shì shénme chá?
A：这是什么茶？

Zhè shì pǔ'ěrchá.
B：这是普洱茶。

Hǎohē ma?
A：好喝吗？

Nǐ dào yìdiǎnr chángchang.
B：你倒一点儿尝尝。

À, zhēn hǎohē.
A：啊，真好喝。

What kind of tea is this

A: What's this?

B: It is tea.

A: What kind of tea is this?

B: It's Pu'er tea.

A: Is it good to drink?

B: You can try some.

A: Oh, it's delicious.

二 生词 New Words

1	想	xiǎng	动	to want
2	吃	chī	动	to eat
3	一点儿	yìdiǎnr		a little; a bit; some
4	什么	shénme	代	what
5	饿	è	形	hungry
6	有点儿	yǒudiǎnr	副	somewhat; rather; a bit
7	这些	zhèxiē	代	these
	这	zhè	代	this; these
	些	xiē	量	some; a few
8	是	shì	动	to be (am, is, are, etc.)
9	饺子	jiǎozi	名	Chinese dumpling
10	那	nà	代	that; those
11	包子	bāozi	名	steamed stuffed bun
12	好吃	hǎochī	形	delicious
13	买	mǎi	动	to buy
14	尝	cháng	动	to taste
15	吧	ba	助	*used at the end of an imperative sentence to soften the tone*
16	啊	à	叹	(*used to express admiration or surprise*) ah; O; oh
17	茶	chá	名	tea
18	普洱茶	pǔ'ěrchá	名	Pu'er tea
19	好喝	hǎohē	形	good to drink
20	倒	dào	动	to pour

三 注释 Notes

（一）怎么问（2）：用疑问代词询问 Interrogation (2): Questions with interrogative pronouns

用“谁”“什么”“哪”询问人或事物。

Asking about somebody or something with “谁”, “什么” or “哪”.

用“哪儿（哪里）”“什么地方”询问处所。

Asking about some place with “哪儿（哪里）” or “什么地方”.

用“怎么”“怎么样”“怎样”询问性质、状态、方式和程度。

Asking about the nature, state, mode or degree with “怎么”, “怎么样” or “怎样”.

用“几”“多少”询问数量。

Asking about the quantity with “几” or “多少”.

例如：

1. A：她是谁？
   B：她是玛丽。
2. A：你要去哪儿？
   B：我去中国。
3. A：你去中国做什么？
   B：我去中国留学。
4. A：你是哪国人？
   B：我是美国（德国 / 日本 / 法国……）人。
5. A：你今天几节课？
   B：今天六节课。
6. A：你一星期多少节课？
   B：二十多节呢。

（二）你想吃（一）点儿什么？ What would you like to eat?

汉语口语中，量词前的“一”常常省略。例如：

The “一” before the classifier is often omitted in spoken Chinese, e.g.,

你吃点儿什么？＝你吃一点儿什么？

我吃个包子。＝我吃一个包子。

四 练习 Exercises

（一）朗读 Read aloud

1. 朗读下列发音相近的词语 Read aloud the following words and expressions with similar pronunciation

xiǎng hē 想 喝	xiánghé 祥和	jiǎozi 饺子	jiāozǐ 骄子
shénme 什么	shēn ma 深 吗	hē chá 喝 茶	héchá 核查
lǜchá 绿茶	lǐ fà 理 发	hǎohē 好喝	hàokè 好客
nǎxiē 哪些	nàxiē 那些	hǎochī 好吃	hǎoshì 好事

2. 朗读下列带轻声的词语 Read aloud the following words with the neutral tones

bāozi 包子	jiǎozi 饺子	zòngzi 粽子	zhǒngzi 种子
wàzi 袜子	shuāzi 刷子	kùzi 裤子	màozi 帽子
jùzi 句子	juànzi 卷子	hézi 盒子	gèzi 个子

3. 朗读下列带三声的词语，注意三声变调 Read aloud the following words and expressions with the 3rd tones and pay attention to the 3rd tone sandhi

zhǐ tīng	zhǐdú	zhǐguǎn	zhǐ jiàn
zhǔbiān	zhǔchí	zhǔyǎn	zhǔbàn

jiǎndān	jiǎnyàn	hǎokàn	hǎohàn
yǔfǎ	yǔsǎn	kěyǐ	biǎoyǎn
mǎi ma	mǎi ba	bǎo le	pǎo le

（二）**替换并朗读** Replace and read aloud

1. A：你饿吗？
   B：有点儿饿。

渴　累　忙　困

2. A：这是什么？
   B：这是饺子。

包子　绿茶　粽子　元宵
糖葫芦　烤白薯

3. A：你想吃点儿什么？
   B：我想吃饺子。

包子　馒头　面包
面条儿　汉堡包　米饭
比萨　三明治

4. A：你想喝点儿什么？
   B：我想喝茶。

矿泉水　咖啡　啤酒
牛奶　可乐　酸奶
果汁

5. A：饺子好吃吗？
   B：很好吃。

包子	好吃
这茶	好喝
这首歌	好听
这个电影	好看
这个字	好写
这篇课文	好读

（**提示**：生词请查阅各类词典。）

（Tip: For new words, please refer to various dictionaries.）

（三）选词填空并朗读下列句子 Choose the appropriate words to fill in the blanks and read aloud the following sentences

1. 是　有　吃　尝尝　真　吗　什么　些

A：你饿________？

B：________点儿饿。

A：你想吃点儿________？

B：这些________什么？

A：这________是饺子。

B：好________吗？

A：买一些________吧。

B：啊，________好吃。

2. 倒　好　吗　茶　什么

A：这是________茶？

B：这是普洱________。

A：好喝________？

B：你________一点儿尝尝。

A：啊，真________喝。

（四）完成下列会话并大声朗读 Complete the following conversations and read them aloud

1. 回答 Answer the questions

（1）A：你饿吗？

B：________________________________。

A：你想吃点儿什么？

B：________________________________。

（2）A：这是什么？

B：________________________________。

A：这是什么茶？

B：________________________________。

A：好喝吗？

B：________________________________。

2. 提问 Ask questions

（1）A：________________________________？

B：我有点儿饿。

A：________________________________？

B：我想吃饺子。

A：________________________________？

B：很好吃。

（2）A：________________________________？

B：这是茶。

A：________________________________？

B：这是普洱茶。

A：________________________________？

B：很好喝。

（五）和同学一起朗读下列会话 Read aloud the following dialogues with your classmates

Nǐ xiǎng jiā ma?
A：你 想 家吗？

Xiǎng. Nǐ ne?
B：想。你 呢？

Wǒ yě xiǎng.
A：我 也 想。

Wǒ xiǎng bàba māma, yě xiǎng jiějie.
B：我 想 爸爸 妈妈，也 想 姐姐。

Wǒ yě shì, wǒ hái xiǎng yéye nǎinai.
A：我 也 是，我 还 想 爷爷 奶奶。

Xiǎng jiā de shíhou, nǐ huì kū ma?
B：想 家的时候，你会哭吗？

Bú huì. Nǐ kū ma?
A：不会。你哭吗？

Yǒushíhou huì.
B：有时候 会。

Nǐ hái xiǎo, cháng gēn tóngxué liáoliao jiù hǎo le.
A：你还小，常 跟同学 聊聊 就好了。

（六）和同学一起表演课文 Act out the text with your classmates

（七）怎么表达 How to express

Wǒ xiǎng...
我想…… I want to...

Wǒ xiǎng dé dào nàge dàxué de jiǎngxuéjīn.
1. 我想得到那个大学的奖学金。

I want to get a scholarship from that university.

Wǒ xiǎng qù Chángchéng kànkan.
2. 我想去长城看看。

I want to see the Great Wall.

（八）朗读中国经典诗词，请注意语音语调 Read aloud the classic Chinese poem and pay attention to the pronunciation and intonation

Wèn Liú Shíjiǔ
问刘十九

[Táng] Bái Jūyì
[唐] 白居易（772—846）

Lǜ yǐ xīn pēi jiǔ, hóng ní xiǎo huǒlú.
绿蚁新醅酒，红泥小火炉。

Wǎn lái tiān yù xuě, néng yǐn yì bēi wú?
晚来天欲雪，能饮一杯无？

（九）请欣赏下列著名的词句 Please enjoy the following well-known saying

Qiānlǐzhīxíng, shǐyúzúxià.

千里之行，始于足下。

A thousand-*li* journey begins with the first step.

Dì-qī kè　　Qǐng nín màn diǎnr shuō

第七课　请您慢点儿说

Lesson 7　Would you please speak more slowly

一 课文 Text

（一）请您慢点儿说

Lǎoshī: Tóngxuémen hǎo! Xiànzài shàng kè. Qǐng kàn hēibǎn / píngmù, qǐng tīng wǒ shuō!

老师：同学们 好！现在 上 课。请 看 黑板 / 屏幕，请 听 我 说！

Xuéshēng: Lǎoshī, qǐng nín màn diǎnr shuō, hǎo ma?

学生：老师，请 您 慢 点儿 说，好 吗？

Lǎoshī: Hǎo de.

老师：好 的。

Would you please speak more slowly

Teacher: Hello, everyone! Now the class begins. Please look at the blackboard/screen! Please listen to me!

Student: Would you please speak more slowly, madam?

Teacher: OK.

（二）您再说一遍，好吗

Lǎoshī: Wǒ xiān shuō yí biàn, qǐng dàjiā gēn wǒ shuō. Dǒngle ma?

老师：我 先 说 一 遍，请 大家 跟 我 说。…… 懂了吗？

Xuéshēng: Lǎoshī, wǒ bù dǒng. Nín zài shuō yí biàn, hǎo ma?

学生：老师，我不 懂。您 再 说 一 遍，好 吗？

Lǎoshī: Hǎo de! Wǒ zài shuō yí biàn, qǐng gēn wǒ shuō. Dǒngle ma?

老师：好 的！我再 说 一 遍，请 跟 我 说。…… 懂了吗？

Xuéshēng: Dǒng le.

学生：懂 了。

Could you say that again, please

Teacher: Let me say it first. Please repeat it after me...Do you understand?

Student: I don't understand, madam. Would you mind saying it again?

Teacher: All right! I say it again. Repeat after me, please...Now do you understand?

Student: Yes, I do.

（三）这个字怎么读

Xuéshēng: Zhège zì zěnme dú?
学生： 这个字怎么读？

Lǎoshī: Dú "qǐng". Qǐng gēn wǒ shuō: Qǐng jìn! Qǐng zuò! Qǐng hē chá! Dǒngle ma?
老师： 读"qǐng（请）"。请跟我说：请进！请坐！请喝茶！懂了吗？

Xuéshēng: Dǒng le.
学生： 懂了。

How do you pronounce this word

Student: How do you pronounce this word, please?

Teacher: It is pronounced as "qǐng". Say them after me. Come in, please! Sit down, please! Have a cup of tea, please! Do you understand?

Student: Yes, I do.

（四）"panda"汉语怎么说

Xuéshēng: Lǎoshī, Yīngyǔ de "panda" Hànyǔ zěnme shuō?
学生： 老师，英语的"panda"汉语怎么说？

Lǎoshī: Hànyǔ shuō "xióngmāo".
老师： 汉语说"熊猫"。

Xuéshēng: Xièxie lǎoshī!
学生： 谢谢老师！

Lǎoshī: Bú xiè. Xiànzài bùzhì zuòyè, qǐng dàjiā yùxí shēngcí hé kèwén. Xiàkè.
老师： 不谢。现在布置作业，请大家预习生词和课文。下课。

Xuéshēng: Lǎoshī, zàijiàn!
学生： 老师，再见！

Lǎoshī: Zàijiàn!
老师： 再见！

How do you say "panda" in Chinese

Student: How do you say "panda" in Chinese, madam?

Teacher: It says "xióngmāo" in Chinese.

Student: Thank you, madam.

Teacher: Don't mention it. Now it's your homework. Please preview the new words and the text. Class is over.

Student: Goodbye, madam!

Teacher: Goodbye!

二 生词 New Words

1	请	qǐng	动	please
2	您	nín	代	you (honorific)
3	慢	màn	形	slow
4	说	shuō	动	to speak; to talk
5	同学	tóngxué	名	schoolmate; classmate
6	现在	xiànzài	名	now
7	上课	shàng kè	动	to give a lesson
8	看	kàn	动	to look; to watch
9	黑板	hēibǎn	名	blackboard
10	屏幕	píngmù	名	screen
11	听	tīng	动	to listen
12	再	zài	副	again
13	遍	biàn	量	(*for actions*) once through; one time
14	大家	dàjiā	代	everyone
15	懂	dǒng	动	to understand
16	读	dú	动	to read
17	怎么	zěnme	代	how

18 进	jìn	动	to come in
19 坐	zuò	动	to sit
20 英语	Yīngyǔ	名	English
21 熊猫	xióngmāo	名	panda
22 布置	bùzhì	动	to assign
23 作业	zuòyè	名	homework
24 预习	yùxí	动	(of students) to prepare lessons before class
25 生词	shēngcí	名	new word
26 课文	kèwén	名	text

三 注释 Notes

（一）您 You (honorific)

"您"是人称代词"你"的敬称。例如："谢谢您，叔叔！""王老师，您好！"

"您" is the honorific appellation of the personal pronoun "你", eg, "谢谢您，叔叔!" or "王老师，您好!".

（二）回答别人感谢可以说"不客气"，也可以说"不谢""不用谢"等。You can say "不客气", "不谢" or "不用谢", etc. to reply to someone's thanks.

四 练习 Exercises

（一）**朗读** Read aloud

1. 朗读下列发音相近的词语 Read aloud the following words and expressions with similar pronunciation

lǎoshī 老师	lǎoshi 老实	tóngxué 同学	dōngxuě 冬雪
xiànzài 现在	xiàndài 现代	shàng kè 上 课	shāngkē 商科
zhùyì 注意	zhǔyi 主意	fā yīn 发 音	fāyán 发言
shēngdiào 声调	shēnzào 深造	yìbiān 一边	yí biàn 一遍

2. 朗读下列教师课堂常用的指令 Read aloud the following instructions teachers often use in class

Dú kèwén, Yào dà shēng lǎngdú. Zuì shǎo yào dú shí biàn.
（1）读课文，要大声 朗读。最少要读十遍。
Read the text, and read it aloud. Read it at least ten times.

Yùxí xīn kè de shēngcí, yào huì dú / niàn.
（2）预习新课的生词，要会读 / 念。
Preview the new words of the new lesson. You should be able to pronounce them.

Qǐng kàn yíxiàr zhùshì.
（3）请 看一下儿注释。
Please read the notes.

（二）**替换并朗读** Replace and read aloud

1. 老师：请看黑板 / 屏幕！

课文	拼音
生词	注释
练习	英文注释

2. 老师：请<u>听我说</u>。

听我发音	再听一遍
跟我读	跟我说
跟我写	

3. 学生：老师，请您<u>慢点儿说</u>。

再说一遍	再读一遍
再解释一下儿	举个例子

4. 学生：这个<u>字</u>怎么<u>读</u>？

音	发	词	念
字	写	句子	翻译

5. 学生：英语的“<u>please</u>”汉语怎么说？
老师：汉语说“<u>请</u>”。

listen/ 听	speak/ 说
read/ 读	write/ 写
translate/ 翻译	grammar/ 语法

（三）选词填空并朗读下列句子 Choose the appropriate words to fill in the blanks and read aloud the following sentences

看　上　发　不　预习　跟　说　个

1. 同学们好！现在________课。
2. 请________黑板 / 屏幕！请听我说！
3. 老师，请您慢点儿________，好吗？
4. 请注意________音，注意声调！
5. 我________懂。您再说一遍，好吗？
6. 这________字怎么读？
7. 请________我说：请进！请坐！请喝茶！懂了吗？
8. 请大家________生词和课文。

（四）和同学一起表演课文 Act out the text with your classmates

（五）怎么表达 How to express

qǐngqiú(1)
请求（1） requesting; asking (1)

Qǐng bǎ chuānghu dǎ kāi / guānshang, hǎo ma?
1. 请 把 窗户 打 开/ 关上，好 吗？

Open/shut the window, will you?

Bù hǎoyìsi, wǒ méi tīngdǒng. Qǐng nǐ zài chóngfù yí biàn, hǎo ma?
2. 不好意思，我没 听懂。请 你再 重复 一 遍，好 吗？

Sorry, but I don't understand. Will you kindly repeat it?

（六）朗读中国经典诗词，请注意语音语调 Read aloud the classic Chinese poem and pay attention to the pronunciation and intonation

Quàn Xué
劝 学

[Táng] Yán Zhēnqīng
［唐］ 颜 真卿（709—784）

Sāngēng dēnghuǒ wǔgēng jī, zhèng shì nán'ér dú shū shí.
三更 灯火 五更 鸡，正 是 男儿 读 书 时。
Hēi fà bù zhī qín xué zǎo, bái shǒu fāng huǐ dú shū chí.
黑发不知 勤 学 早，白 首 方 悔 读 书 迟。

（七）请欣赏下列著名的词句 Please enjoy the following well-known saying

Yǒu zhì zhě shì jìng chéng.
有 志 者 事 竟 成。

Where there is a will, there is a way.

Dì-bā kè
第八课
Lesson 8

Nǐ zhēn yǒu yǎnguāng
你真有眼光
You are a man of vision

一 课文 Text

（一）你真有眼光

Nǐ yào qù nǎr?
A：你要去哪儿？

Wǒ yào qù Zhōngguó.
B：我要去中国。

Nǐ shì qù lǚxíng ma?
A：你是去旅行吗？

Bú shì.
B：不是。

Nǐ qù zuò shénme?
A：你去做什么？

Wǒ qù liú xué.
B：我去留学。

Nǐ xuéxí Hànyǔ ma?
A：你学习汉语吗？

Duì!
B：对！

Nǐ zhēn yǒu yǎnguāng!
A：你真有眼光！

Xièxie nín, shūshu.
B：谢谢您，叔叔。

You are a man of vision

A: Where are you going?

B: I'm going to China.

A: Are you planning to travel there?

B: No.

A: What are you going to do in China?

B: I'm going to study there.

A: Are you going to learn Chinese?

B: Yes!

A: You are a man of vision.

B: Thank you, Uncle.

（二）别怕难

（爸爸跟儿子 / 女儿视频）

Nǐ xuéxí máng ma?
A：你学习忙吗？

Bú tài máng.
B：不太忙。

Hànyǔ nán ma?
A：汉语难吗？

Tǐng nán de.
B：挺难的。

Bié pà nán, háizi! Bù chī kǔ zhōng kǔ, nán yǒu tián shàng tián.
A：别怕难，孩子！不吃苦中苦，难有甜上甜。

Wǒ dǒng le, bàba.
B：我懂了，爸爸。

Don't be afraid of difficulties

(The father is having a video chat with his son/daughter)

A: Are you busy studying?

B: No, not too busy.

A: Is Chinese difficult?

B: Yes, it's rather difficult.

A: Don't be afraid of difficulties, child! No pains, no gains.

B: I understand, Dad.

二 生词 New Words

1 眼光 yǎnguāng 名 eye; sight; vision

2 旅行	lǚxíng	动	to travel
3 做	zuò	动	to do
4 留学	liú xué	动	to study abroad
5 叔叔	shūshu	名	uncle
6 儿子	érzi	名	son
7 女儿	nǚ'ér	名	daughter
8 忙	máng	形	busy
9 太	tài	副	too; extremely; much too
10 难	nán	形	difficult
11 挺	tǐng	副	very; rather; quite
12 别	bié	副	don't
13 怕	pà	动	to be afraid of
14 吃苦	chī kǔ	动	to suffer hardships
苦	kǔ	形	bitter; painful
15 中	zhōng	名	inside
16 甜	tián	形	sweet

专名 Zhuānmíng Proper Noun

中国	Zhōngguó	China

三 注释 Notes

(一) er 和儿化韵 The retroflex er and the r-ending retroflexion

1. 卷舌韵母 The retroflex er

发 er 时，先把舌位放在发 e 的位置，然后将舌尖轻轻上翘，同时发音。例如：

To pronounce er, first put the tongue in the position for e, and then slightly curl up the tip of the tongue, e.g.,

értóng	érzi	ěrsāi	èrbǎi
儿童	儿子	耳塞	二百
children	son	earphones	two hundred

2. 儿化韵 The r-ending retroflexion

er 可与其他的韵母结合成一个儿化韵母。儿化韵的写法是在原韵母之后加 r，汉字写法是在原汉字之后写个“儿”字。例如：

The final er can be combined with another final to form an r-ending final. In transcription, it is shown by adding an r to the original final. In Chinese characters, it is represented by adding the character “儿” after the original character, e.g.,

nǎr	zhèr	wánr	huàr
哪儿	这儿	玩儿	画儿
where	here	to play	picture

（二）**挺（副）** very; rather; quite

“挺”也是程度副词，但比“很”的程度略低，口语中常与后边的动词或形容词组成“挺……的”结构。例如：

“挺” is also an adverb of degree, but it is slightly lower than “很” in degree. In spoken Chinese, it is often followed by a verb or adjective to form the “挺……的” structure, e.g.,

1. 汉字挺难的。
2. 我挺忙的。
3. 你爸爸身体挺好的。

四 练习 Exercises

（一）朗读 Read aloud

1. 朗读下列发音相近的词语 Read aloud the following words and expressions with similar pronunciation

yǎnguāng 眼光	yàn guāng 验 光	lǚxíng 旅行	lìxíng 例行
liú xué 留 学	liúxuè 流血	xuéxí 学习	xuéqī 学期
Hànyǔ 汉语	Hányǔ 韩语	shūshu 叔叔	shǔ shù 数 数
bié pà 别怕	bié pá 别爬	tǐng nán de 挺 难 的	tǐng lán de 挺 蓝 的

2. 朗读下列带儿化韵的词语 Read the following words and expressions with the r-ending retroflexion

qù nǎr 去哪儿	qù nàr 去那儿	zài nǎr 在哪儿	zài zhèr 在这儿
huà huàr 画 画儿	hǎowánr 好玩儿	hǎibiānr 海边儿	pángbiānr 旁边儿
dōngbianr 东边儿	xībianr 西边儿	nánbianr 南边儿	běibianr 北边儿
zuǒbianr 左边儿	yòubianr 右边儿	qiánbianr 前边儿	hòubianr 后边儿
shàngbianr 上边儿	xiàbianr 下边儿	lǐbianr 里边儿	wàibianr 外边儿

（二）替换并朗读 Replace and read aloud

1. A：你去哪儿？
   B：我去<u>中国</u>。

美国	德国
法国	英国
泰国	日本

2. A：你去做什么？

B：去留学。

旅行	讲学
访问	考察
经商	比赛

小词典

讲学	jiǎng xué	动	to give lectures
访问	fǎngwèn	动	to visit
考察	kǎochá	动	to investigate
经商	jīng shāng	动	to be in business
比赛	bǐsài	动	to have a contest

（三）**选词填空并朗读下列句子** Choose the appropriate words to fill in the blanks and read aloud the following sentences

留学　中国　去　学习　有　什么

1. A：你要________哪儿？

B：我要去________。

2. A：你去中国做________？

B：我去中国________。

3. A：你________汉语吗？

B：对！

4. 你真________眼光。

中　难　挺　太　忙　别

1. A：你学习________吗？

B：不________忙。

2. A：汉语________吗？

B：________难的！

3. ________怕难！不吃苦________苦，难有甜上甜。

（四）和同学一起表演课文 Act out the text with your classmates

（五）怎么表达 How to express

gǔlì(1)
鼓励（1） encouraging (1)

Bié xiè qì, jiāyóu!
1. 别泄气，加油！

Don't be discouraged. Carry on!

Bié hàipà shuō Hànyǔ.
2. 别害怕说汉语。

Don't be afraid to speak Chinese.

（六）朗读中国经典诗词，请注意语音语调 Read aloud the classic Chinese poem and pay attention to the pronunciation and intonation

Juéjù
绝句

[Táng] Dù Fǔ
［唐］杜甫（712—770）

Liǎng gè huánglí míng cuì liǔ, yì háng báilù shàng qīngtiān.
两个黄鹂鸣翠柳，一行白鹭上青天。

Chuāng hán Xī Lǐng qiānqiū xuě, mén bó Dōng Wú wàn lǐ chuán.
窗含西岭千秋雪，门泊东吴万里船。

（七）请欣赏下列著名的词句 Please enjoy the following well-known saying

Tiān shēng wǒ cái bì yǒu yòng.
天生我材必有用。

Heaven has bestowed genius on us; he will also find its use some day.

Dì-jiǔ kè 第九课 Lesson 9

Bú pà, jiù bù juéde nán 不怕，就不觉得难

If you are not afraid, you won't find it difficult

一 课文 Text

（一）我知道，你们都很忙

（玛丽跟妈妈视频聊天儿）

Mǎlì: Māma, nǐ máng ma?
玛丽：妈妈，你 忙 吗？

Māma: Bú tài máng.
妈妈：不太 忙。

Mǎlì: Bàba máng bu máng?
玛丽：爸爸 忙 不 忙？

Māma: Nǐ bàba hěn máng. Nǐ ne?
妈妈：你爸爸很 忙。你呢？

Mǎlì: Wǒ yě hěn máng.
玛丽：我 也 很 忙。

Māma: À, wǒ zhīdào, nǐmen dōu hěn máng.
妈妈：啊，我 知道，你们 都 很 忙。

I know you're all very busy

(Mary is having a video chat with her mother)

A: Mom, are you busy?

B: No, not too busy.

A: Is Dad busy?

B: Yes, your father is very busy. How about you?

A: I'm busy, too.

B: Ah, I know both of you are very busy.

（二）不怕，就不觉得难

（课堂上）

Lǎoshī: Nǐ lái dú kèwén 《nǐ zhēn yǒu yǎnguāng》.
老师：（对学生 A）你来读 课文《你 真 有 眼光》。

（学生 A 读后）

Lǎoshī: Nǐ hěn bàng! Dúde hěn hǎo!
老师：（对学生 A）你很 棒！读得 很 好！

Xuéshēng A: Xièxie!
学生 A： 谢谢！

Lǎoshī: Nǐ juéde Hànyǔ nán bu nán?
老师： 你觉得 汉语 难 不 难？

Xuéshēng A: Wǒ juéde Hànyǔ bú tài nán, dàn yě bù róngyì.
学生 A： 我觉得汉语不太难，但 也不容易。

Xuéshēng B: Bù, Hànyǔ hěn nán.
学生 B： 不，汉语 很 难。

Lǎoshī: Nǐ bú pà, jiù bù juéde nán; pà, jiù juéde nán.
老师：（对学生 B）你不怕，就不 觉得 难；怕，就觉得难。

Xuéshēng B: Shì ma?
学生 B： 是吗？

Lǎoshī: Shìde!
老师： 是的！

If you're not afraid, you won't find it difficult

(In class)

Teacher: (To Student A) Please read aloud the text "You are a man of vision".

(After Student A finishes reading it)

Teacher: (To Student A) You are great! Well read!

Student: Thanks!

Teacher: Do you find Chinese difficult?

Student A: I don't think Chinese is too difficult, but it's not easy, either.

Student B: I don't think so. Chinese is very difficult.

Teacher: (To Student B) If you are not afraid, you won't find it difficult. If you are afraid, you will find it difficult.

Student B: Really?

Teacher: Yes!

二 生词 New Words

1	知道	zhīdào	动	to know; to be aware of
2	就	jiù	副	if that is the case, then
3	觉得	juéde	动	to feel; to think
4	来	lái	动	to come
5	棒	bàng	形	great; excellent
6	得	de	助	*used between a verb or an adjective and its complement to indicate the result or degree*
7	但	dàn	连	but
8	容易	róngyì	形	easy

三 注释 Notes

（一）怎么问（3）：正反问句 Interrogation (3): Affirmative-negative questions

把谓语主要成分的肯定式与否定式并列起来提问，即构成正反问句。例如：

An affirmative-negative question is one in which the affirmative and negative forms of the main element of the predicate are paralleled, e.g.,

1. A：你觉得汉语难不难？

   B：不太难，但也不容易。

2. A：你去不去公园？

   B：去。/ 不去。

3. A：爸爸忙不忙？

   B：他很忙。

（二）啊，你们都很忙。Ah, you're all very busy.

叹词“啊”的音较长，表示“明白了”“知道了”的意思。

The exclamation “啊” is pronounced relatively long, which means “I see” or “I understand”.

四 练习 Exercises

（一）朗读 Read aloud

1. 朗读下列发音相近的词语 Read aloud following words and expressions with similar pronunciation

hěn bàng 很 棒	hěn pàng 很 胖	hěn máng 很 忙	hěn màn 很 慢
xièxie 谢谢	xiēxie 歇歇	juéde 觉得	jiè de 借的
shìpín 视频	shípǐn 食品	zhīdào 知道	chídào 迟到

2. 朗读下列带轻声的词语 Read aloud the following words and expressions with the neutral tones

nǐmen 你们	tāmen 他们	è ma 饿吗	kě ma 渴 吗
hóng de 红 的	huáng de 黄 的	bái de 白 的	hēi de 黑 的
lán de 蓝 的	lǜ de 绿 的	fěn de 粉 的	zǐ de 紫 的

3. 朗读下列带半三声的词语 Read aloud the following words and expressions with the half 3rd tones

hěn gāo 很 高	hěn nán 很 难	hěn dà 很 大	hǎo ba 好 吧
nǐ hē 你喝	nǐ lái 你来	mǐfàn 米饭	hǎo le 好 了
běn bān 本 班	běnlái 本来	hǎo liáng 好 凉	hǎo tàng 好 烫
Běijīng 北京	xuěshān 雪山	jǐngsè 景色	hǎokàn 好看

（二）替换并朗读 Replace and read aloud

1. A：爸爸忙不忙？
   B：你爸爸很忙。

哥哥	弟弟
姐姐	妹妹

2. A：你觉得汉语难吗？
   B：我觉得汉语不太难，但也不容易。

英语	日语
法语	阿拉伯语
西班牙语	俄语

（三）选词填空并朗读下列句子 Choose the appropriate words to fill in the blanks and read aloud the following sentences

就　得　不　也　都　太

1. 他课文读________很好。
2. 我觉得汉语不________难，但也不容易。
3. 老师说："你不怕，________不觉得难；怕，________觉得难。"
4. 我跟妈妈视频聊天儿，我问爸爸忙________忙，妈妈说，爸爸很忙。
5. 妈妈问我忙不忙，我说，我________很忙。
6. 啊，我知道，你们________很忙。

（四）完成下列会话并大声朗读 Complete the conversations and read them aloud

1. 回答 Answer the questions

   A：妈妈，你忙吗？
   B：____。
   A：爸爸忙不忙？
   B：____。

2. 提问 Ask questions

A：________________________________？

B：不太忙。

A：________________________________？

B：你爸爸很忙。

A：________________________________？

B：我觉得汉语不太难，但也不容易。

（五）你是 A，请你向 B 提问 Suppose you are A and ask questions to B

A：________________________________？

B：我觉得汉语发音不太难。

A：________________________________？

B：我觉得汉字很难。

A：________________________________？

B：我不怕。

（六）根据实际情况回答问题 Answer the questions according to the actual situations

1. 你预习生词和课文吗？
2. 你怕听写吗？
3. 你读课文吗？
4. 你读得怎么样？
5. 你觉得汉语难不难？
6. 你怕难吗？

（七）和同学一起表演课文 Act out the text with your classmates

（八）怎么表达 How to express

kànwàng
看望 calling on; visiting; seeing

Nǐ jīntiān hǎoxiē le ma?
1. A：你今天 好些了吗？

Are you better today?

Wǒ gǎnjué hǎoduō le.
B：我 感觉 好多 了。

I'm much better now.

Zhè huār shì sòng nǐ de, xīwàng nǐ xǐhuan.
2. A：这 花儿是 送 你的，希望 你 喜欢。

These flowers are for you. I hope you will like them.

Duō měi de huār a! Xièxie nǐ.
B：多 美 的 花儿 啊！谢谢 你。

How beautiful these flowers are! Thank you very much.

（九）朗读中国经典诗词，请注意语音语调 Read aloud the classic Chinese poem and pay attention to the pronunciation and intonation

Zhú Shí
竹石

[Qīng] Zhèng Xiè
［清］ 郑 燮（1693—1765）

Yǎodìng qīngshān bú fàngsōng, lì gēn yuán zài pò yán zhōng.
咬定 青山 不 放松，立 根 原 在 破岩 中。
Qiān mó wàn jī hái jiānjìng, rèn ěr dōng xī nán běi fēng.
千 磨 万 击 还 坚劲，任 尔 东 西 南 北 风。

（十）请欣赏下列著名的词句 Please enjoy the following well-known saying

Sān rén xíng, bì yǒu wǒ shī.
三 人 行，必 有 我 师。

Where there are three men walking together, one of them must be qualified to be my teacher.

Dì-shí kè
第十课 Lesson 10

Wǒ xiǎng gēn nín yìqǐ zhào gè xiàng
我想跟您一起照个相 I want to take a picture with you

一 课文 Text

Wǒ xiǎng gēn nín yìqǐ zhào gè xiàng
我想跟您一起照个相

Wǒ lái jièshào yíxiàr, zhè shì Wáng lǎoshī. Lǎoshī, zhè shì wǒ péngyou.
A：我来介绍一下儿，这是王老师。老师，这是我朋友。

Lǎoshī hǎo!
B：老师好！

Nǐmen hǎo!
C：你们好！

Lǎoshī, wǒ xiǎng gēn nín yìqǐ zhào gè xiàng, hǎo ma?
A：老师，我想跟您一起照个相，好吗？

Hǎo a.
C：好啊。

Yòng wǒ de shǒujī pāi ba.
A：（对B）用我的手机拍吧。

Yī, èr, sān, hǎo! Nǐ kàn zěnmeyàng?
B：一、二、三，好！（对A）你看怎么样？

Zhēn hǎo! Xièxie lǎoshī!
A：真好！谢谢老师！

Bú kèqi!
C：不客气！

I want to take a picture with you

A: Let me make an introduction. This is Mr. Wang. Madam, this is my friend.

B: Hello, madam!

C: How do you do?

A: Madam, I want to take a picture with you, okey?

C: All right.

A: (To B) You can take pictures with my mobile phone.

B: One, two, three, okay! (To A) How do you think of it?

A: It's nice! Thank you, madam!

C: You're welcome!

二 生词 New Words

1	照相	zhào xiàng	动	to take a picture
2	介绍	jièshào	动	to introduce
3	一下儿	yíxiàr		(*used after a verb as its complement, indicating an act or an attempt*) one time
4	朋友	péngyou	名	friend
5	用	yòng	动	to use
6	手机	shǒujī	名	mobile phone
	手	shǒu	名	hand
	机	jī		machine
7	拍	pāi	动	to take (a picture); to shoot
8	看	kàn	动	to think; to consider

三 注释 Notes

(一) 老师，我想跟您一起照（一）个相，好吗？ Madam, I want to take a picture with you, okey?

也可以说："老师，我想跟您一起照（一）张相，好吗？" 口语中量词前的"一"常常省略。

You can also say “老师，我想跟您一起照（一）张相，好吗？”. The “一” before the quantifier is often omitted in spoken Chinese.

（二）我来介绍一下儿。Let me make an introuduction.

“一下儿”是动量补语，表示动作时间短。

“一下儿” is a complement of frequency, indicating the duration of an action is short.

四 练习 Exercises

（一）朗读 Read aloud

1. 朗读下列发音相近的词语 Read aloud the following words and expressions with similar pronunciation

zhào xiàng 照 相	zhāoyáng 朝阳	jièshào 介绍	jiēdào 街道
shǒujī 手机	shōují 收集	pāi zhào 拍 照	páizhào 牌照
kànkan 看看	kǎnkǎn 侃侃	zěnyàng 怎样	zhēn liàng 真 亮

2. 朗读下列带三声的词语，注意三声变调 Read aloud the following words with the 3rd tones and pay attention to the 3rd tone sandhi

jiǎndān 简单	jiǎnbiàn 简便	biǎoyáng 表扬	biǎoyǎn 表演
jiǎnchá 检查	lǚxíng 旅行	yǔfǎ 语法	lǐ fà 理 发
bǐsài 比赛	děngdài 等待	biǎoshì 表示	gǎnxiè 感谢
nǎinai 奶奶	ěrduo 耳朵	yǐzi 椅子	sǎngzi 嗓子

（二）**替换并朗读** Replace and read aloud

1. 我来介绍一下儿，这是王老师。

我爸爸	我妈妈	我朋友
我姐姐	我弟弟	我同学

2. A：你看怎么样？
   B：真好！

不错	棒
美	有眼光

（三）**选词填空并朗读下列句子** Choose the appropriate words to fill in the blanks and read aloud the following sentences

得　　跟　　介绍　　拍　　看

1. 我来________一下儿，这是王老师。老师，这是我朋友。
2. 老师，我想________您一起照个相，好吗？
3. 用我的手机________吧。
4. 你________怎么样？
5. 我看照________很好。

（四）**完成下列会话并大声朗读** Complete the following conversations and read them aloud

1. A：我来介绍一下儿，这是王老师。老师，这是我朋友。
   B：______________________________！
   C：你们好！
2. A：______________________________？
   C：好啊。
3. A：用我的手机拍吧！
   B：______________________________？
   A：真好！

（五）**和同学一起表演课文** Act out the text with your classmates

（六）怎么表达 How to express

bù hǎoyìsi
不好意思 sorry

Bù hǎoyìsi, ràng nǐ jiǔ děng le.
1. A：不 好意思，让 你久 等 了。

Sorry to have kept you waiting.

Méi guānxi.
B：没 关系。

That's all right.

Dǎrǎo nín le, bù hǎoyìsi.
2. A：打扰 您 了，不好意思。

Sorry to have disturbed you.

Méi shénme.
B：没 什么。

It's nothing.

（七）朗读中国经典诗词，请注意语音语调 Read aloud the classic Chinese poem and pay attention to the pronunciation and intonation

Jīnlǚyī
金缕衣

[Táng] Wúmíngshì
［唐］ 无名氏

Quàn jūn mò xī jīnlǚyī, quàn jūn xī qǔ shàonián shí.
劝 君 莫 惜 金缕衣，劝 君 惜 取 少年 时。
Huā kāi kān zhé zhí xū zhé, mò dài wú huā kōng zhé zhī.
花 开 堪 折 直 须 折，莫 待 无 花 空 折 枝。

（八）请欣赏下列著名的词句 Please enjoy the following well-known saying

Dú shū bǎi biàn, ér yì zì xiàn.
读 书 百 遍，而义自 见。

Read a book a hundred times, and its import becomes obvious.

Dì-shíyī kè

第十一课 Lesson 11

Nǐ hē hóngchá háishi lǜchá

你喝红茶还是绿茶 Would you like black tea or green tea

一 课文 Text

Nǐ hē hóngchá háishi lǜchá
你喝 红茶 还是绿茶

（A、B、C 在一起聊天儿）

Nǐmen kě ma?
A：你们 渴吗？

Kě.
B：渴。

Wǒ yě hěn kě.
C：我 也 很渴。

Nǐmen xiǎng hē diǎnr shénme?
A：你们 想 喝点儿 什么？

Wǒ xǐhuan hē kāfēi, gěi wǒ yì bēi kāfēi ba.
B：我 喜欢 喝咖啡，给 我 一 杯 咖啡 吧。

Gěi nǐ.
A：给你。

Xièxie!
B：谢谢！

Bú kèqi!
A：不客气！

Nǐ ne?
B：（问 C）你呢？

Wǒ bù cháng hē kāfēi, wǒ xiǎng hē bēi chá.
C：我不 常 喝咖啡，我 想 喝杯茶。

Nǐ hē hóngchá háishi lǜchá?
A：你喝 红茶 还是 绿茶？

Hē lǜchá ba.
C：喝绿茶吧。

Gěi nǐ, zhè kě shì zhēnzhèng de Xī Hú lóngjǐng.
A：给你，这 可是 真正 的西湖 龙井。

À, zhēn hǎohē!
C：啊，真 好喝！

Would you like black tea or green tea

(A, B and C are chatting together...)

A: Are you thirsty?

B: Yes, I am.

C: I'm very thirsty, too.

A: What would you like to drink?

B: I like coffee. Give me a cup of coffee, please.

A: Here you are.

B: Thank you!

A: You're welcome!

B: (To C) What about you?

C: I don't drink coffee very often. I'd like a cup of tea.

A: Would you like black tea or green tea?

C: Green tea, please.

A: Here you are. It's the real Longjing tea from the west lake.

C: Oh, it's really tasty!

二 生词 New Words

1	红茶	hóngchá	名	black tea
2	还是	háishi	连	or
3	绿茶	lǜchá	名	green tea
4	在	zài	副	*used to indicate an action in progress*
5	喜欢	xǐhuan	动	to like; to be fond of
6	咖啡	kāfēi	名	coffee

7 给	gěi	动	to give
8 杯	bēi	名、量	cup
9 常	cháng	副	often
10 可	kě	副	*used in a declarative sentence for emphasis*
11 可是	kě shì		*used for emphasis*
12 真正	zhēnzhèng	形	real

专名 Zhuānmíng Proper Noun

西湖	Xī Hú	West Lake (one of China's most famous lakes in Hangzhou)

三 注释 Notes

(一) 怎么问（4）：选择问句（……还是……？）Interrogation (4): Alternative questions with "……还是……?"

用"还是"连接两种（或多种）可能来提问，要求选择其中一项作答。例如：

"还是" is used to connect two (or more) possibilities for the listener to choose from, e.g.,

1. A：你喝绿茶还是红茶？

   B：绿茶吧。

2. A：你的手机是新的还是旧的？

   B：新的。

3. A：这是你哥哥还是你弟弟？

   B：这是我弟弟。

（二）怎么问（5）：省略问句（……呢？）Interrogation (5): Elliptical questions with "……呢？"

省略问句有两种用法：

An elliptical question can be used in two ways:

1. 在没有上下文的情况下，问的是处所。例如：

Without a specific context, it refers to the location of someone or something, e.g.,

（1）我的书呢？（=我的书在哪儿？）

（2）你的车呢？（=你的车在哪儿？）

2. 有上下文时，根据上下文判断要回答的内容。例如：

If there is a context, the reference is dependent on the context, e.g.,

（1）A：我喝咖啡，你呢？（=你喝什么？）

B：我喝茶。

（2）A：麦克是美国人，马丁呢？（=马丁是哪国人？）

B：不知道。

四 练习 Exercises

（一）朗读 Read aloud

1. 朗读下列发音相近的词语 Read aloud the following words and expressions with similar pronunciation

háishi 还是	háizi 孩子	hěn kě 很渴	hěn è 很饿
kèqi 客气	kěqì 可气	hǎohē 好喝	hǎo gēr 好歌儿
yì bēi 一杯	yí bèi 一倍	kě shì 可是	kèshí 课时

2. 声调搭配 Collocations of tones

huídá 回答	tóngxué 同学	míngnián 明年	liú xué 留学

niúnǎi 牛奶	píjiǔ 啤酒	yóu yǒng 游 泳	ménkǒu 门口
xuéxiào 学校	xíguàn 习惯	búyào 不要	chídào 迟到
biéde 别的	péngyou 朋友	juéde 觉得	máfan 麻烦

3. 多音节连读 Polysyllabic liaison

chī mántou 吃 馒头	chī mǐfàn 吃米饭	chī jiǎozi 吃 饺子	
chī bāozi 吃包子	chī miànbāo 吃 面包	chī hànbǎobāo 吃 汉堡包	
hē kāfēi 喝咖啡	hē niúnǎi 喝牛奶	hē píjiǔ 喝啤酒	hē lǜchá 喝绿茶

4. 朗读下列词语，注意“一”的变调 Read aloud the following words and pay attention to the tone sandhi of “一”

yì bēi 一杯	yì méi 一枚	yìbiān 一边	yí piàn 一片
yì pán 一盘	yì wǎn 一碗	yídào 一道	yímiàn 一面
yì tiáo 一条	yìdiǎnr 一点儿	yìshēn 一身	yí jiàn 一件
yì hé 一盒	yì bāo 一包	yì shǒu 一 手	yí gè 一个

5. 朗读下列词语，注意“不”的变调 Read aloud the following words and expressions and pay attention to the tone sandhi of “不”

bù chī 不吃	bù hē 不喝	bù shuō 不说	bù duō 不多
bù lái 不来	bùxíng 不行	bù tóng 不同	bù néng 不能
bù lěng 不冷	bù dǎ 不打	bù hǎo 不好	bù xiǎo 不小
bú qù 不去	bú pà 不怕	bú zuò 不做	bú è 不饿

6. 朗读下列带轻声的词语 Read aloud the following words with the neutral tones

xiāngzi 箱子	guìzi 柜子	jiāzi 夹子	jiàzi 架子
jiǎnzi 剪子	qiánzi 钳子	jìngzi 镜子	shūzi 梳子
diézi 碟子	pánzi 盘子	bēizi 杯子	bèizi 被子
bózi 脖子	bízi 鼻子	wūzi 屋子	yuànzi 院子

（二）替换并朗读 Replace and read aloud

1. A：你渴吗？
   B：我很渴。

饿	累	忙
冷	困	热

2. A：你喝红茶还是喝绿茶？
   B：喝绿茶吧。

茶 / 咖啡	啤酒 / 水
果汁 / 牛奶	可乐 / 雪碧

3. 啊，真好喝。

好吃	好看	好听
好玩儿	好闻	

4. A：茶好喝吗？
   B：很好喝。

咖啡	热	很热
水	凉	不凉
菜	辣	不辣
包子	咸	不咸
饺子	淡	有点儿淡
酸奶	酸	不酸

5. A：你常<u>喝茶</u>吗？

B：常<u>喝茶</u>。/ 不常<u>喝茶</u>。

喝酒	上网	听音乐
踢足球	散步	锻炼

（三）选词填空并朗读下列句子 Choose the appropriate words to fill in the blanks and read aloud the following sentences

渴　还是　的　吗　喝　常　什么　杯

1. A：你们渴________？

B：我很________。

2. 你想喝点儿________？

3. 我喜欢喝咖啡，请给我一________咖啡吧。

4. 我不________喝咖啡，我想喝杯茶。

5. A：你喝红茶________绿茶？

B：喝绿茶。

6. A：这可是真正________西湖龙井。

B：啊，真好________。

（四）完成下列会话并大声朗读 Complete the following conversations and read them aloud

A：你渴吗？

B：____。

A：你想喝点儿什么？

B：____。

A：你喝红茶还是绿茶？

B：____。

A：给你，这可是真正的西湖龙井。

B：____。

（五）根据实际情况回答问题 Answer the questions according to the actual situations

1. 你常和朋友聊天儿吗？
2. 你喜欢喝茶还是咖啡？

（六）和同学一起表演课文 Act out the text with your classmates

（七）读后说 Read the passage and say it

那天，我和朋友一起在山本她们房间聊天儿，我们都很渴。山本问我们想喝点儿什么，玛丽说她想喝一杯咖啡。我说，我不常喝咖啡，我想喝杯茶。山本问我想喝红茶还是绿茶，我说喝绿茶。山本给我一杯绿茶，她说，这可是真正的西湖龙井。啊，真好喝。

（八）怎么表达 How to express

shāngliang
商量 consulting; talking over

Wǒmen yìqǐ chū qu chī wǎnfàn hǎo ma?
1. 我们 一起 出 去吃 晚饭 好 吗？

Would you like to go out for dinner with me?

Zhège zhōumò gēn wǒ qù chāoshì mǎi dōngxi hǎo ma?
2. 这个 周末 跟 我去 超市 买 东西好 吗？

Would you like to go shopping with me at the supermarket this weekend?

（九）朗读中国经典诗词，请注意语音语调 Read aloud the classic Chinese poem and pay attention to the pronunciation and intonation

Mǐn Nóng qí èr
悯 农（其二）

[Táng] Lǐ Shēn
[唐] 李 绅（772—846）

Chú hé rì dāng wǔ, hàn dī hé xià tǔ.
锄禾日当午，汗滴禾下土。
Shéi zhī pán zhōng cān, lì lì jiē xīnkǔ.
谁知盘中餐，粒粒皆辛苦。

（十）请欣赏下列著名的词句 Please enjoy the following well-known saying

Zàijiā kào fùmǔ, chūmén kào péngyou.
在家靠父母，出门靠朋友。

At home, we depend on our parents.

When we leave home, we need friends to help us.

Dì-shí'èr kè

第十二课 Lesson 12

Nǐ xiǎng qù Chángchéng ma

你想去 长城 吗

Do you want to go to the Great Wall

一 课文 Text

（一）你想去长城吗

（A 和 B 在看手机里的图片）

Zhè jiù shì Chángchéng ba?

A：这就是 长城 吧？

Shì. Nǐ xiǎng qù Chángchéng ma?

B：是。你 想 去 长城 吗？

Xiǎng qù.

A：想 去。

Zhǎo gè zhōumò zánmen yìqǐ qù, hǎo ma?

B：找 个周末 咱们 一起去，好 吗？

Hǎo a, zánmen zěnme qù ne?

A：好啊，咱们 怎么 去 呢？

Zuò gāotiě qù, zěnmeyàng?

B：坐 高铁去，怎么样？

Hǎo!

A：好！

Do you want to go to the Great Wall

(A and B are looking at the pictures on the mobile phone)

A: Is this the Great Wall?

B: Yes. Do you want to go to the Great Wall?

A: Yes, I do.

B: Let's go to the Great Wall some weekend, shall we?

A: OK, how can we get there?

B: Let's go by high-speed railway, shall we?

A: OK!

（二）这就是古老的汉字

Nǐ kàn, zhè shì shénme?
A：你看，这是什么？

Bù zhīdào.
B：不知道。

Nǐ kàn tāmen xiàng shénme?
A：你看它们 像 什么？

À, zhège xiàng tàiyáng, zhège xiàng yuèliang, zhège xiàng rén.
B：啊，这个 像 太阳，这个 像 月亮，这个 像 人。

Duì, zhè jiù shì gǔlǎo de Hànzì.
A：对，这就是古老的汉字。

Shì ma? Zhèxiē dōu shì shénme zì?
B：是吗？这些 都 是 什么 字？

Zhège shì "rì" zì, zhè shì "yuè" zì, zhè shì "rén" zì.
A：这个是"日"字，这是"月"字，这是"人"字。

À, zhēn xiàng.
B：啊，真 像。

Nǐ kàn zhège shì shénme zì?
A：（指"明"）你看 这个是 什么 字？

Wǒ bú rènshi.
B：我不认识。

"Rì" hé "yuè" zài yìqǐ, huì zěnmeyàng ne?
A："日"和"月"在一起，会 怎么样 呢？

Huì hěn míngliàng, duì ma?
B：会很 明亮，对 吗？

Duì ya! Zhè jiù shì "míngliàng" de "míng" zì.
A：对呀！这 就是"明亮"的"明"字。

À! Zhēn yǒu yìsi.
B：啊！真 有意思。

These are ancient Chinese characters

A: Look, what's this?

B: I don't know.

A: What do you think they are like?

B: Ah, this is like the sun, this is like the moon, and this is like a man.

A: Yes, these are ancient Chinese characters.

B: Really? What characters are they?

A: This is the "sun", this is the "moon", and this is the "person".

B: Ah, they look so alike.

A: (Pointing at "明") What do you think this character is?

B: I don't know it.

A: What happens if the sun and the moon are together?

B: It'll be bright, right?

A: That's right! This is the character "bright".

B: Ah! Chinese characters are so interesting.

（三）这些字我也会写

Nǐ juéde Hànyǔ nán ma?
A：你 觉得汉语 难 吗？

Fā yīn bú tài nán, Hànzì bǐjiào nán.
B：发 音不太难，汉字比较 难。

Nǐ kàn wǒ zěnme xiě.
A：你看 我怎么写。

（写"一、二、三、人、大、太、天"）

À! Zhèxiē zì hěn jiǎndān, wǒ yě huì xiě.
B：啊！这些字很 简单，我也会写。

Zhè jǐ gè zì nǐ dōu huì xiě ba?
A：（指"日""月""明"）这几个字你都 会写吧？

Méi wèntí.
B：没 问题。

I can write these characters, too

A: Do you find Chinese difficult?

B: The pronunciation is not too difficult, but Chinese characters are rather difficult.

A: See me write these characters.

(Writing "一，二，三，人，大，太，天")

B: Ah! These characters are very simple. I can write them, too.

A: (Pointing at “日”, “月” and “明”) Can you write all these characters?

B: No problem.

二 生词 New Words

1	图片	túpiàn	名	photograph
2	就	jiù	副	exactly; precisely
3	找	zhǎo	动	to look for; to try to find
4	周末	zhōumò	名	weekend
5	咱们	zánmen	代	we
6	高铁	gāotiě	名	high-speed railway
7	古老	gǔlǎo	形	ancient; old
8	汉字	Hànzì	名	Chinese character
9	它们	tāmen	代	they
10	像	xiàng	动	to be like
11	太阳	tàiyáng	名	sun
12	月亮	yuèliang	名	moon
13	认识	rènshi	动	to know
14	和	hé	连	and
15	明亮	míngliàng	形	bright
16	呀	ya	助	*used instead of* 啊 *after a syllable ending in* a, e, i, *or*, ü
17	明	míng		bright
18	有意思	yǒu yìsi		interesting; enjoyable
	意思	yìsi	名	interest; fun

19 会	huì	动	to be able to
20 写	xiě	动	to write
21 比较	bǐjiào	副、动	rather; relatively; to compare
22 简单	jiǎndān	形	simple
23 没问题	méi wèntí		no problem
没(有)	méi (yǒu)	动、副	not to have; not
问题	wèntí	名	question; problem

专名 Zhuānmíng Proper Noun

长城	Chángchéng	the Great Wall

三 注释 Notes

"我们"和"咱们""我们" and "咱们"

"我们"可以称呼对话双方，也可以称呼对话双方的自己一方。"咱们"只能总称对话双方。例如：

"我们" can be used to refer to both sides of a dialogue, or to the side of the speaker. "咱们" can only be used to refer to the two sides of the dialogue, e.g.,

1. 你是美国人，我是泰国人。咱们/我们都是留学生。
2. 你们是留学生，我们是中国学生，咱们是同学。

不能说：* 你们是留学生，咱们是中国学生，我们是同学。

四 练习 Exercises

（一）朗读 Read aloud

1. 朗读下列发音相近的词语 Read aloud the following words and expressions with similar pronunciation

jiùshì 就是	jiǔshí 九十	Hànzì 汉字	hànzi 汉子
zhège 这个	zhè gēr 这歌儿	yuèliang 月亮	yuè yáng 越洋
zhēnxiàng 真相	zhēn xiāng 真香	xiǎng qù 想去	xiǎngqǐ 想起

2. 朗读下列带三声的词语，注意三声变调 Read aloud the following words and expressions with the 3rd tones and pay attention to the 3rd tone sandhi

nǐ shuō 你说	nǐ lái 你来	nǐ mǎi 你买	nǐ kàn 你看	wǒ de 我的
hǎochī 好吃	hǎowánr 好玩儿	hǎo měi 好美	hǎokàn 好看	hǎo de 好的
měi tiān 每天	měi nián 每年	měihǎo 美好	kǔ liàn 苦练	hǎo ma 好吗
yǎnguāng 眼光	yǎnqián 眼前	lǐxiǎng 理想	lǐniàn 理念	yǎnjing 眼睛

3. 朗读下列带轻声的词语 Read aloud the following words and expressions with the neutral tones

qiántou 前头	hòutou 后头	zhǐtou 指头	zhěntou 枕头
zǒu ma 走吗	zǒu ba 走吧	qù ma 去吗	qù ba 去吧
lái ma 来吗	lái ba 来吧	mǎi ma 买吗	mǎi ba 买吧
hǎowánr ma 好玩儿吗	hǎokàn ma 好看吗	hǎochī ma 好吃吗	hǎohē ma 好喝吗

（二）**替换并朗读** Replace and read aloud

1. A：你想去<u>长城</u>吗？
   B：想去。

上海	西安	公园
超市	动物园	图书馆

2. A：咱们怎么去呢？
   B：咱们<u>坐高铁</u>去吧。

坐公交车	开车	坐飞机
打的	骑车	走路

（**提示**：生词请查阅各类词典。）

(For new words, please refer to various dictionaries.)

（三）**选词填空并朗读下列句子** Choose the appropriate words to fill in the blanks and read aloud the following sentences

个　坐　想　去

1. 你________去长城吗？
2. 我________周末咱们一起去，好吗？
3. 好啊，咱们怎么________呢？
4. ________高铁去，怎么样？

比较　也　觉得

1. 你________汉语难吗？
2. 发音不太难，汉字________难。
3. 啊！这些字很简单，我________会写。

（四）完成下列会话并大声朗读 Complete the following conversations and read them aloud

1. 回答 Answer the questions

A：周末你想去哪儿？

B：____。

A：你想怎么去？

B：____。

2. 提问 Ask questions

A：____？

B：“日”“月”“明”这三个字我都会写。

A：____？

B：我觉得汉字很难。

（五）和同学一起朗读下面的会话 Read aloud the following conversation with your classmates

A：（指“人”“木”）你看，这是什么字？

B：这是“人”字，这是“木”字。

A：（指“休”）这个呢？

B：不知道。

A：木，就是树（shù，tree）。人很累（lèi，tired），他坐在树下做什么呢？

B：他休息呢。

A：对。这就是休息的“休”字。

B：啊，真有意思。

（六）根据实际情况回答问题 Answer the questions according to the actual situations

1. 你觉得汉语的发音难不难？声调呢？
2. 你现在一分钟能读多少个字？
3. 你一分钟能写多少个字？
4. 你觉得汉语有意思吗？

（七）你是 A，请你向 B 提问 Suppose you are A and ask questions to B

A：________________________________？

B：我觉得汉语不太难。

A：________________________________？

B：有的音我不会发。

A：________________________________？

B：我的声调不好。

A：________________________________？

B：难，但我不怕。

A：________________________________？

B：我会 / 不会用汉语问路（读课文、写汉字、查词典、用筷子）。

（八）和同学一起表演课文 Act out the text with your classmates

（九）读后说 Read the passage and say it

今天，我跟朋友一起看长城的照片，我问他想不想去长城看看。他说，来中国最想去看的，一是长城，二是大熊猫。

我们想找个周末，坐高铁去看长城。

（十）怎么表达 How to express

dāying 答应 agreement; promise

Nǐ gěi wǒ fǔdǎo fǔdǎo, hǎo ma?
A：你给我辅导辅导，好吗？

Could you give me some guidance?

Hǎo! / Xíng! / Kěyǐ! / Méi wèntí.
B：好！/ 行！/ 可以！/ 没 问题。

All right! / No problem.

（十一）朗读中国经典诗词，请注意语音语调 Read aloud the classic Chinese poem and pay attention to the pronunciation and intonation

Chú Zhōu Xī Jiàn
滁州西涧

[Táng] Wéi Yìngwù
[唐] 韦 应物（约 737—791）

Dú lián yōu cǎo jiàn biān shēng, shàng yǒu huánglí shēn shù míng.
独怜幽草涧边生，上有黄鹂深树鸣。

Chūn cháo dài yǔ wǎn lái jí, yě dù wú rén zhōu zì héng.
春潮带雨晚来急，野渡无人舟自横。

（十二）请欣赏下列著名的词句 Please enjoy the following well-known saying

Bú dào Chángchéng fēi hǎohàn.
不到 长城 非好汉。

One who fails to reach the Great Wall cannot be called a true man.

Dì-shísān kè

第十三课 Lesson 13

Kěyǐ jiā nǐ de wēixìn ma

可以加你的微信吗 Can I add you on WeChat

一 课文 Text

（一）可以加你的微信吗

Qǐngwèn, nín guìxìng?

A：请问，您贵姓？

Wǒ xìng Lǐ.

B：我姓李。

Nǐ jiào shénme míngzi?

A：你叫什么名字？

Wǒ jiào Lǐ Dàtóng. Nǐ jiào shénme míngzi?

B：我叫李大同。你叫什么名字？

Wǒ jiào Mǎdīng. Zhōngwén míngzi jiào Xiè Zhōngwén. Nǐ yě shì liúxuéshēng ma?

A：我叫马丁。中文名字叫谢钟文。你也是留学生吗？

Wǒ bú shì liúxuéshēng, wǒ shì Zhōngguó xuéshēng. Nǐ shì nǎ guó rén?

B：我不是留学生，我是中国学生。你是哪国人？

Wǒ shì Měiguórén. Nǐ xuéxí shénme zhuānyè?

A：我是美国人。你学习什么专业？

Wǒ xué wàimào. Nǐ xuéxí shénme zhuānyè?

B：我学外贸。你学习什么专业？

Wǒ xuéxí xiàndài Hànyǔ. Rènshi nǐ hěn gāoxìng.

A：我学习现代汉语。认识你很高兴。

Wǒ yě hěn gāoxìng.

B：我也很高兴。

Kěyǐ jiā nǐ de wēixìn ma?

A：可以加你的微信吗？

Dāngrán kěyǐ.
B：当然 可以。

Wǒ xǐhuan jiāo péngyou.
A：我喜欢 交 朋友。

Nà tài hǎo le. Péngyou duōle lù hǎo zǒu ma.
B：那太好了。朋友 多了路好走嘛。

Can I add you on WeChat

A: May I have your surname, please?

B: My surname is Li.

A: What is your name?

B: My name is Li Datong. What is your name?

A: My name is Martin. My Chinese name is Xie Zhongwen. Are you an overseas student, too?

B: No, I'm not an overseas student. I'm a Chinese student. What nationality are you?

A: I'm American. What's your major?

B: I study foreign trade. What's your major?

A: I study modern Chinese. Nice to meet you.

B: Nice to meet you, too.

A: Can I add you on WeChat?

B: Of course.

A: I like making friends.

B: That would be great. If we have more friends, we will have less difficulties.

（二）你知道他的手机号吗

（桌子上有一把钥匙）

Āi, zhè shì shéi de yàoshi?
C：哎，这 是 谁 的 钥匙？

À, shì Mǎdīng de, tā gāng zǒu.
B：啊，是 马丁 的，他 刚 走。

Kuài gěi tā dǎ gè diànhuà. Nǐ zhīdào tā de shǒujīhào ma?
C：快 给他 打个 电话。你 知道 他的 手机号 吗？

Zhīdào, wǒ dǎ tā de shǒujī. Wèi, Mǎdīng ma?
B：知道，我打他的手机。喂，马丁 吗？

Shì, Dàtóng Lǐ, nǐ yǒu shénme shìr ma?
A：是，大同 李，你有 什么 事儿吗？

Wǒ jiào Lǐ Dàtóng, bú jiào Dàtóng Lǐ.
B：我叫 李大同，不 叫 大同 李。

À, duìbuqǐ. Nǐ yǒu shénme shìr?
A：啊，对不起。你有 什么事儿？

Nǐ de yàoshi hái zài zhèr ne!
B：你的钥匙 还在这儿呢！

À, hǎo, wǒ qù ná.
A：啊，好，我去拿。

Nǐ zài nǎr ne?
B：你在哪儿呢？

Wǒ jiù zài lóu xià, nǐ cóng chuāngkǒu rēng gěi wǒ ba.
A：我就在楼下，你从 窗口 扔给我吧。

Hǎo de. Jiēzhù!
B：好的。接住！

Xièxie nǐ!
A：谢谢你！

Bú kèqi.
B：不客气。

Do you know his cell phone number

(There is a key on the table)

C: Hey, whose key is this?

B: Oh, it's Martin's. He's just left.

C: Phone him right now. Do you know his cell phone number?

B: Yes. I'll call him on his cell phone. Hi, Martin?

A: Hello, Datong Li. What's the matter?

B: My name is Li Datong, not Datong Li.

A: Oh, I'm sorry. What's up?

B: Your key is still here!

A: Ah, yes. I'll go to get it.

B: Where are you?

A: I'm just downstairs. You can throw it to me through the window.

B: All right. Catch it!

A: Thank you!

B: You're welcome.

二 生词 New Words

1	可以	kěyǐ	助动	may; can
2	加	jiā	动	to add
3	微信	wēixìn	名	WeChat
4	请问	qǐngwèn	动	excuse me
5	贵姓	guìxìng	名	one's (honorable) surname
	贵	guì		honorable
	姓	xìng	名	surname
6	叫	jiào	动	to call; to name
7	名字	míngzi	名	name; first name
8	中文	Zhōngwén	名	Chinese (language)
9	留学生	liúxuéshēng	名	overseas student
10	专业	zhuānyè	名	major; speciality
11	外贸	wàimào	名	foreign trade
12	现代	xiàndài	形	modern
13	高兴	gāoxìng	形	happy
14	当然	dāngrán	副	of course
15	交	jiāo	动	to associate with; to befriend
16	路	lù	名	way; road
17	好	hǎo	形	easy (to do)
18	走	zǒu	动	to walk; to go
19	嘛	ma	助	*indicating that something is obvious*
20	号	hào	名	number
21	桌子	zhuōzi	名	table; desk

22	把	bǎ	量	*for something with a handle*
23	钥匙	yàoshi	名	key
24	谁	shéi	代	who; whom
25	刚	gāng	副	just
26	快	kuài	副	hurry up
27	给	gěi	介	(*used to introduce the recipient of an action*) for; to
28	打	dǎ	动	to phone
29	电话	diànhuà	名	phone
30	事儿	shìr	名	thing; matter; affair
31	还	hái	副	still
32	拿	ná	动	to take
33	楼下	lóu xià		downstairs
	楼	lóu	名	tower; storeyed building
	下	xià	名	low position or rank
34	从	cóng	介	from
35	窗口	chuāngkǒu	名	window
36	扔	rēng	动	to throw
37	接	jiē	动	to catch
38	住	zhù	动	*used as a complement after a verb, indicating a steadiness or firmness*

专名 Zhuānmíng Proper Nouns

1	李大同	Lǐ Dàtóng	a name of person
2	马丁	Mǎdīng	a name of person

3 谢钟文 Xiè Zhōngwén a name of person

4 美国 Měiguó U.S.A

三 注释 Notes

（一）贵姓 One's (honorable) surname

询问他人姓时用的敬辞。

"贵姓" is a respectful way of asking someone's surname.

（二）中国人的姓和名 The family names and given names of Chinese people

中国人的姓在前，名在后。姓多为一个汉字，如"李""王""张""梁"等，名多为一个汉字或两个汉字。如：李大同，"李"是姓，"大同"是名；吴丹，"吴"是姓，"丹"是名。

In China, the family name comes before the given name. The family name is usually one Chinese character, e.g., "李", "王", "张", "梁", etc. The given name is usually one or two Chinese characters. For example: in "李大同", "李" is the family name, and "大同" is the given name; in "吴丹", "吴" is the family name, and "丹" is the given name.

姓	名
李	大同
吴	丹
王	伟国

（三）外贸 Foreign trade

"对外贸易"的简称。

"外贸" is short for "对外贸易".

四 练习 Exercises

（一）朗读 Read aloud

1. 朗读下列发音相近的词语 Read aloud the following words and expressions with similar pronunciation

qǐngwèn 请问	qīnwěn 亲吻	zhuānyè 专业	zhuǎnyè 转业
gāoxìng 高兴	háoqíng 豪情	rènshi 认识	rénshì 人事
kěyǐ 可以	kèyì 刻意	yàoshi 钥匙	yàoshì 要事
wēixìn 微信	wéixīn 违心	jiēzhù 接住	jièzhù 借助

2. 朗读下列带三声变调的词语 Read aloud the following words and expressions with the 3rd tones sandhi

qǐng chī 请 吃	qǐng hē 请 喝	qǐng tīng 请 听	qǐng shuō 请 说
hěn hóng 很 红	hěn téng 很 疼	hěn màn 很 慢	hěn luàn 很 乱
hǎo lěng 好 冷	hǎo dǒng 好 懂	měihǎo 美好	lǎoxiǎo 老小

3. 朗读下列带轻声的词语 Read aloud the following words and expressions with the neutral tones

hǎo ma 好吗	duì ma 对吗	dǒng ma 懂 吗	huì ma 会吗
hǎo le 好了	duì le 对了	dǒng le 懂 了	huì le 会了
zhème 这么	nàme 那么	zěnme 怎么	duōme 多么

（二）**替换并朗读** Replace and read aloud

1. A：你叫什么名字？
   B：我叫<u>李大同</u>。
   A：你是哪国人？
   B：我是<u>中国</u>人。

马丁	美国
玛丽	英国
山本	日本
李贞贤	韩国

2. A：你学习什么专业？
   B：我学习<u>汉语</u>。

外贸	英语	日语
法语	西班牙语	

3. A：这是谁的手机？
   B：这是<u>我</u>的手机。

他　李大同　马丁　老师

（三）**选词填空并朗读下列句子** Choose the appropriate words to fill in the blanks and read aloud the following sentences

哪　外贸　好　名字　当然　高兴　是　什么

1. 请问，您叫什么________？你也________留学生吗？
2. 我不是留学生，我是中国学生。你是________国人？
3. 我是美国人。你学习________专业？
4. A：我学________。你学习什么专业？
   B：我学习现代汉语。
5. A：很________认识你。可以加你的微信吗？
   B：________可以。
6. A：我喜欢交朋友。
   B：那太好了，朋友多了路________走嘛。

还　从　事儿　在　走　给

1. A：这是谁的钥匙？
   B：啊，是马丁的。他刚________。
2. A：快________他打个电话。你知道他的手机号吗？
   B：知道，我打他的手机。
3. 李大同，你有什么________吗？
4. A：你的钥匙________在这儿呢！
   B：啊，我去拿。
5. A：你在哪儿呢？
   B：我就________楼下。
6. 我________窗口扔给你吧。

（四）根据实际情况回答问题 Answer the questions according to the actual situations

1. 你叫什么名字？
2. 你是哪国人？
3. 你学习什么专业？
4. 你都有什么课？
5. 你们有几个老师？
6. 你们的老师叫什么名字？

（五）和同学一起表演课文 Act out the text with your classmates

（六）读后说 Read the passage and say it

我叫……，我是……人。我学习汉语。我觉得汉语的发音不太难，汉字非常难。他/她是我的中国朋友，他/她叫……。他/她学习外贸专业。我喜欢交朋友，因为朋友多了路好走。

（七）怎么表达 How to express

wènhòu
问候 regards; greetings

Nǐ zěnme le?
1. A：你怎么了？
What's wrong with you?

Wǒ tóu yǒudiǎnr téng.
B：我头有点儿疼。
I have a headache.

Nǐ jīntiān hǎo diǎnr le ma?
2. A：你今天好点儿了吗？
Are you feeling better today?

Wǒ juéde hǎo diǎnr le.
B：我觉得好点儿了。
I feel a little better.

（八）朗读中国经典诗词，请注意语音语调 Read aloud the classic Chinese poem and pay attention to the pronunciation and intonation

Yè Yǔ Jì Běi
夜雨寄北

[Táng] Lǐ Shāngyǐn
［唐］李 商隐（813—858）

Jūn wèn guīqī wèi yǒu qī, Bā Shān yè yǔ zhǎng qiū chí.
君问归期未有期，巴山夜雨涨秋池。
Hé dāng gòng jiǎn xī chuāng zhú, què huà Bā Shān yè yǔ shí.
何当共剪西窗烛，却话巴山夜雨时。

（九）请欣赏下列著名的词句 Please enjoy the following well-known saying

Sìhǎi zhīnèi jiē xiōngdì.
四海之内皆兄弟。

All men are brothers within the four seas.

Dì-shísì kè

第十四课 Lesson 14

Nǐ māma zuò shénme gōngzuò

你妈妈做什么工作 What does your mother do

一 课文 Text

（一）你妈妈做什么工作

Nǐ bàba shì lǎoshī ma?

A：你爸爸是老师吗？

Bú shì, tā bú shì lǎoshī, tā shì dàifu.

B：不是，他不是老师，他是大夫。

Nǐ māma zuò shénme gōngzuò?

A：你妈妈做什么工作？

Wǒ māma shì hùshi.

B：我妈妈是护士。

What does your mother do

A: Is your father a teacher?

B: No, he isn't. He is a doctor.

A: What does your mother do?

B: My mother is a nurse.

（二）这个手机是谁的

Āi, zhège shǒujī shì shéi de? Shì nǐ de ma?

A：哎，这个手机是谁的？是你的吗？

Bú shì, wǒ de zài zhèr ne. Wǒ de shì Huáwéi de, bú shì Píngguǒ de. Wǒ de shì lán de, bú shì bái de.

B：不是，我的在这儿呢。我的是华为的，不是苹果的。我的是蓝的，不是白的。

Nà zhège shǒujī shì shéi de ne?

A：那这个手机是谁的呢？

Kěnéng shì Mǎdīng de, tā de shǒujī shì Píngguǒ de.
B：可能是马丁的，他的手机是苹果的。

Mǎdīng zài nǎr ne?
A：马丁在哪儿呢？

Tā zài nàbiān ne. Nǐ kàn, tā zài zhǎo shénme ne?
B：他在那边呢。你看，他在找什么呢？

Mǎdīng, zhè shì bu shì nǐ de shǒujī?
A：马丁，这是不是你的手机？

Shì. Āiyā, wǒ zhèng zhǎo tā ne.
C：是。哎呀，我正找它呢。

Gěi nǐ.
A：给你。

Xièxie!
C：谢谢！

Bú kèqi.
A：不客气。

Whose cell phone is this

A: Hey, whose cell phone is this? Is it yours?

B: No, mine is here. Mine is a Huawei phone, not an iPhone. Mine is blue, not white.

A: So whose cell phone is it?

B: This could be Martin's. His is an iPhone.

A: Where is Martin?

B: There he is. Look, what is he looking for?

A: Martin, is this your cell phone?

C: Yes. Oh dear, I was just looking for it.

C: Here you are.

B: Thank you!

A: You're welcome.

二 生词 New Words

1	工作	gōngzuò	名、动	job; to work
2	大夫	dàifu	名	doctor

	医生	yīshēng	名	doctor
3	护士	hùshi	名	nurse
4	这儿	zhèr	代	here
5	蓝	lán	形	blue
6	白	bái	形	white
7	可能	kěnéng	副	possibly; probably
8	那边	nàbiān	代	there
9	哎呀	āiyā	叹	(*used to express surprise*) wow; gee; my
10	正	zhèng	副	just; right; exactly

专名 Zhuānmíng Proper Nouns

1	华为	Huáwéi	Huawei
2	苹果	Píngguǒ	Apple

三 注释 Notes

“的”字短语 The “的”-phrase

“的”字短语是由“的”字附在名词、代词、形容词、动词等实词或短语后边组成的，其作用相当于名词，可以充当名词能充当的句子成分。例如：

The “的”-phrase is formed by attaching the particle “的” to a noun, pronoun, adjective, verb or phrase. Its grammatical function is equal to that of a noun, e.g.,

1. A：这个手机是谁的？
   B：是我的。
2. A：这是谁的手机？
   B：可能是马丁的。
3. 我的是华为的，不是苹果的。我的在这儿呢。
4. 他的手机是黑的。

四 练习 Exercises

(一) 朗读 Read aloud

1. 朗读下列发音相近的词语 Read aloud the following words and expressions with similar pronunciation

hùshi 护士	hūshì 忽视	kěnéng 可能	hénéng 核能
shǒujī 手机	shōují 收集	nǎr 哪儿	nàr 那儿
Píngguǒ 苹果	bīngguo 冰过	Huáwéi 华为	huàwéi 化为

2. 朗读下列带三声的词语，注意三声变调 Read aloud the following words and expressions with the 3rd tones and pay attention to the 3rd tone sandhi

hǎotīng 好听	hǎoshuō 好说	hǎojǐng 好景	hǎokàn 好看
hǎoduō 好多	háorén 好人	hǎoshòu 好受	hǎogǎn 好感
hǎochù 好处	hǎoguò 好过	hǎodǎi 好歹	hǎoxiàng 好像
hǎohàn 好汉	hǎopíng 好评	hǎobǐ 好比	hǎoyì 好意

3. 朗读下列带轻声的词语 Read aloud the following words and expressions with the neutral tones

mùtou 木头	shítou 石头	kǔtour 苦头儿	tiántour 甜头儿
déle 得了	suànle 算了	zhāohu 招呼	xiàngsheng 相声
juéde 觉得	jìde 记得	miǎnde 免得	xiǎnde 显得
lǎnde 懒得	shěngde 省得	dǒngde 懂得	shěde 舍得

（二）替换并朗读 Replace and read aloud

1. A：你爸爸是老师吗？
   B：不是，他是<u>大夫</u>。
   A：你妈妈做什么工作？
   B：我妈妈是<u>护士</u>。

工程师	老师
司机	家庭主妇
商人	大夫
警察	记者

2. A：这是你的<u>手机</u>吗？
   B：是。/ 不是。

书	词典	钥匙
卡	本子	眼镜

小词典

工程师	gōngchéngshī	名	engineer
司机	sījī	名	driver
商人	shāngrén	名	businessman
警察	jǐngchá	名	police
家庭	jiātíng	名	family
主妇	zhǔfù	名	housewife
记者	jìzhě	名	reporter

（三）选词填空并朗读下列句子 Choose the appropriate words to fill in the blanks and read aloud the following sentences

谁　的　那　找　可能　手机　在　哪儿

1. A：这是你________手机吗？
   B：不是，这不是我的手机。我的是蓝的，不是白的。我的________这儿呢。
2. A：那这是________的手机呢？
   B：________是马丁的，他的手机是白的。

3. A：马丁在________呢？

B：他在________边呢。

4. A：马丁，这是不是你的________？

B：是，哎呀，我正________它呢。

（四）**完成下列会话并大声朗读** Complete the following conversations and read them aloud

1. A：你爸爸也是老师吗？

B：________，________________。

A：你妈妈做什么工作？

B：________________________。

2. A：这是你的手机吗？

B：________。________________。

A：那这是谁的手机呢？

B：________________________。

A：马丁在哪儿呢？

B：________________________。

A：马丁，这是你的手机吗？

B：________________________。

（五）**你是A，请你向B提问** Suppose you are A and ask questions to B

A：________________________？（几）

B：我家有五口人。

A：________________________？（是）

B：我爸爸是老师。

A：________________________？（做　什么）

B：我妈妈是大夫。

A：________________________？

B：我没有哥哥和弟弟，我只有一个姐姐。

（六）**根据实际情况回答问题** Answer the questions according to the actual situations

1. 你家有几口人？
2. 你有哥哥 / 姐姐 / 弟弟 / 妹妹吗？
3. 你爸爸做什么工作？你妈妈呢？
4. 你还想家吗？
5. 想家的时候，你怎么办？

（七）**和同学一起表演课文** Act out the text with your classmates

（八）**读后说** Read the passage and say it

我的家

我家有五口人：爸爸、妈妈、哥哥、妹妹和我。我爸爸是医生，每天工作很忙。我妈妈是家庭主妇，哥哥大学毕业后去美国读研究生，妹妹上高中。我是来中国学汉语的留学生。

来中国后，我常常想爸爸妈妈，也想哥哥妹妹。所以，我常常跟他们视频聊天儿，告诉他们我在中国留学的情况。我说，我学得很好，生活也没问题，让他们放心。

（九）**怎么表达** How to express

> qǐngjiào
> 请教 asking for advice; consulting

Kěyǐ xiàng nǐ qǐngjiào yí gè wèntí ma?
1. 可以 向 你 请教 一个问题 吗？

May I ask you a question?

Nǐ zhīdào zhège zěnme yòng ma?
2. A：你 知道 这个 怎么 用 吗？

Do you know how it works?

Zhīdào, wǒ lái jiāo nǐ.
B：知道，我来 教 你。

Yes. I'll show you.

（十）朗读中国经典诗词，请注意语音语调 Read aloud the classic Chinese poem and pay attention to the pronunciation and intonation

Xún Yǐnzhě Bú Yù
寻 隐 者 不 遇

[Táng] Jiǎ Dǎo
[唐] 贾 岛（779—843）

Sōng xià wèn tóngzǐ, yán shī cǎi yào qù.
松 下 问 童子，言 师 采 药 去。

Zhǐ zài cǐ shān zhōng, yún shēn bù zhī chù.
只 在此 山 中，云 深 不 知 处。

（十一）请欣赏下列著名的词句 Please enjoy the following well-known saying

Jǐ suǒ bú yù, wù shī yú rén.
己 所 不 欲，勿 施 于人。

Do not do to others as you would not be done by.

Dì-shíwǔ kè

第十五课 Lesson 15

Nǐ hěn yǒu zhìqì

你很有志气 You have high aspirations

一 课文 Text

Nǐ hěn yǒu zhìqì

你很有志气

Nǐ měi tiān shàngwǔ、xiàwǔ dōu yǒu kè ma?

A：你每天上午、下午都有课吗？

Bù, wǒ zhōu'èr hé zhōusì shàngwǔ、xiàwǔ dōu yǒu kè, zhōuyī、zhōusān、zhōuwǔ zhǐ shàngwǔ yǒu kè, xiàwǔ méi kè.

B：不，我周二和周四上午、下午都有课，周一、周三、周五只上午有课，下午没课。

Nǐ zhǐ xué Hànyǔ ma?

A：你只学汉语吗？

Bù, wǒ xué Hànyǔ, yě xué shūfǎ hé huà huàr, hái xué tán pípa、lā èrhú.

B：不，我学汉语，也学书法和画画儿，还学弹琵琶、拉二胡。

Shì ma? Nà nǐ hěn máng ba?

A：是吗？那你很忙吧？

Shì. Wǒ měi tiān dōu hěn máng, yě hěn kuàilè.

B：是。我每天都很忙，也很快乐。

Nǐ Hànyǔ xuéde zěnmeyàng?

A：你汉语学得怎么样？

Wǒ hěn nǔlì, xuéde hái búcuò.

B：我很努力，学得还不错。

Hěn hǎo, nǐ hěn yǒu zhìqì, yě hěn zhēng qì!
A：很好，你很有志气，也很争气！

Nǎlǐ.
B：哪里。

You have high aspirations

A: Do you have classes every morning and afternoon?

B: No. On Tuesday and Thursday, I have classes both in the morning and in the afternoon. On Monday, Wednesday and Friday, I have classes only in the morning and not in the afternoon.

A: Do you only study Chinese?

B: No. Except for Chinese, I also study calligraphy and painting. I learn to play the *pipa* and *erhu* as well.

A: Really? So you are very busy, aren't you?

B: Yes. I am very busy every day, but I am also very happy.

A: How are you getting on with your Chinese?

B: I study very hard, and I'm doing fine.

A: Very good! You have high aspirations, and you have something to show for your efforts.

B: I am flattered.

二 生词 New Words

1	每天	měi tiān		every day
	每	měi	代	every; each; per
	天	tiān	名	day
2	上午	shàngwǔ	名	morning
3	下午	xiàwǔ	名	afternoon
4	周	zhōu	名	week
5	只	zhǐ	副	only
6	书法	shūfǎ	名	calligraphy
7	画	huà	动	to draw; to paint
8	画儿	huàr	名	drawing; painting
9	还	hái	副	also; too

10	弹	tán	动	to play (a musical instrument)
11	琵琶	pípa	名	*pipa* (Chinese string musical instrument with a fretted fingerboard historically with a plectrum, but now mainly with the fingers)
12	拉	lā	动	to play (a musical instrument)
13	二胡	èrhú	名	*erhu* (two-stringed bowed instrument with a low register)
14	快乐	kuàilè	形	happy
15	努力	nǔlì	形	hard-working
16	不错	búcuò	形	not bad
	错	cuò	形	wrong
17	志气	zhìqì	名	aspiration; ambition
18	争气	zhēng qì	动	to make effort to seek self-improvement
19	哪里	nǎlǐ	代	*used when responding politely to a compliment*

三 注释 Notes

(一) 副词“只”“也”“都”“还” The adverbs “只 (only)”, “也 (also)”, “都 (all; both)” and “还” (also)

副词“只”“也”“都”和“还”放在动词或形容词前边，在句中做状语。例如：

The adverbs “只”, “也”, “都” and “还” are placed before verbs or adjectives and function as adverbials, e.g.,

1. 你只学汉语吗？
2. 我学汉语，也学书法和画画儿，还学弹琵琶、拉二胡。
3. 我每天都很忙，也很快乐。

（二）哪里 I'm flattered

常用来婉转地推辞对自己的褒奖。例如：

“哪里” is often used to politely decline a compliment. e.g.,

A：你很有志气。

B：哪里。

四 练习 Exercises

（一）朗读 Read aloud

1. 朗读下列发音相近的词语 Read aloud the following words and expressions with similar pronunciation

nǔlì 努力	núlì 奴隶	shūfǎ 书法	shūfā 抒发
kuàilè 快乐	kuài le 快了	búcuò 不错	bǔ kè 补课
zhìqì 志气	zhījǐ 知己	zhēng qì 争气	zhěng qí 整齐

2. 朗读下列带“不”的词语 Read aloud the following words and expressions with “不”

bù hē 不喝	bù máng 不忙	bù hǎo 不好	búyào 不要
bù tīng 不听	bù xué 不学	bù dǒng 不懂	bú kàn 不看
bù suān 不酸	bù tián 不甜	bù jiǎng 不讲	bú niàn 不念
bù xīn 不新	bùxíng 不行	bù qǐng 不请	bú jìn 不进

（二）替换并朗读 Replace and read aloud

1. A：今天星期几？
   B：星期二。

昨天	星期一
前天	星期日
大前天	星期六
明天	星期三
后天	星期四
大后天	星期五

2. 我学汉语，也学书法和画画儿。

学日语	学法语	外贸
吃米饭	吃包子	饺子
喝咖啡	喝普洱	龙井

（三）选词填空并朗读下列句子 Choose the appropriate words to fill in the blanks and read aloud the following sentences

不错　吧　只　忙　都　怎么样　有　学

1. A：你汉语学得________？
   B：我学习很努力，学得也________。
2. 你很________志气，也很争气！
3. A：你每天上午、下午________有课吗？
   B：不。我周二和周四上午、下午都有课，周一、周三、周五________上午有课，下午没课。
4. A：你只________汉语吗？
   B：不，我学汉语，也学书法和画画儿。
5. A：是吗？那你很忙________？
   B：我每天都很________，也很快乐。

（四）**完成下列会话并大声朗读** Complete the following conversations and read them aloud

A：你每天上午、下午都有课吗？

B：________________________________。

A：你只学汉语吗？

B：________________________________。

A：是吗？那你每天都很忙吧？

B：________________________________。

A：你很努力，也很争气！

B：________________________________。

（五）**你是A，请你向B提问** Suppose you are A and ask questions to B

A：________________________________？

B：我不是每天下午都有课。

A：________________________________？

B：只星期二和星期四下午有课。

A：________________________________？

B：下午没课的时候，我去学书法和画画儿。

A：________________________________？

B：我很忙，也很快乐。

（六）**根据实际情况回答问题** Answer the questions according to the actual situations

1. 你每天上午、下午都有课吗？
2. 你星期几下午有课？
3. 没课的时候你做什么？
4. 你只学汉语吗？
5. 你忙不忙？
6. 你每天过得怎么样？

（七）**和同学一起表演课文** Act out the text with your classmates

（八）读后说 Read the passage and say it

我来中国学汉语，每天上午都有课，我每天都去上课。下午没有课的时候，我去学习书法和画画儿。我学习很努力，学得也不错。

（九）怎么表达 How to express

gǔlì(2)
鼓励（2） encouraging (2)

Bié fàngqì! Jiānchí cái néng chénggōng.
1. 别放弃！坚持才能成功。
Don't give up! If you hang on, you'll succeed.

Jiānchí xiàqu, nǐ yídìng néng xuéhuì.
2. 坚持下去，你一定能学会。
Hang in there, you'll learn it.

Bié shīqù xìnxīn.
3. 别失去信心。
Don't lose confidence.

（十）朗读中国经典诗词，请注意语音语调 Read aloud the classic Chinese poem and pay attention to the pronunciation and intonation

Niǎo Míng Jiàn
鸟鸣涧

[Táng] Wáng Wéi
[唐] 王 维（701—761）

Rén xián guìhuā luò, yè jìng chūn shān kōng.
人闲桂花落，夜静春山空。
Yuè chū jīng shān niǎo, shí míng chūn jiàn zhōng.
月出惊山鸟，时鸣春涧中。

（十一）请欣赏下列著名的词句 Please enjoy the following well-known saying

Jūnzǐ tǎn dàngdàng.
君子坦荡荡。
A gentleman is open and poised.

Dì-shíliù kè

第十六课 Lesson 16

Pútao zěnme mài

葡萄怎么卖 How much are the grapes

一 课文 Text

Pútao zěnme mài

葡萄怎么卖

（在水果店）

Diànzhǔ: Nǐ hǎo! Lái diǎnr shénme?

店主：你好！来点儿什么？

Mǎdīng: Pútao zěnme mài?

马丁：葡萄怎么卖？

Diànzhǔ: Èrshíbā kuài yì jīn.

店主：二十八块一斤。

Mǎdīng: Zhēn guì ya.

马丁：真贵呀。

Diànzhǔ: Shì. Zhè zhǒng pútao shì wàiguó jìnkǒu de, guóchǎn de piányi yìxiē.

店主：是。这种葡萄是外国进口的，国产的便宜一些。

Mǎdīng: Tián ma?

马丁：甜吗？

Diànzhǔ: Zhè liǎng zhǒng pútao dōu tè tián, nǐ kěyǐ chángchang.

店主：这两种葡萄都特甜，你可以尝尝。

Mǎdīng: À, zhēn tián. Lái diǎnr ba, wǒ yào piányi de.

马丁：（尝了一个）啊，真甜。来点儿吧，我要便宜的。

Diànzhǔ: Hái mǎi biéde ma?

店主：还买别的吗？

Mǎdīng: Cǎoméi yì jīn duōshao qián?

马丁：草莓一斤多少钱？

Diànzhǔ: Yì jīn shíwǔ kuài.
店主： 一斤十五 块。

Mǎdīng: Zài mǎi yìxiē cǎoméi hé míhóutáo ba.
马丁： 再 买一些草莓和猕猴桃 吧。

Diànzhǔ: Nǐ yào jǐ gè míhóutáo?
店主： 你要几个 猕猴桃？

Mǎdīng: Lái wǔ gè ba.
马丁： 来 五个吧。

Diànzhǔ: Yígòng bāshí'èr kuài sì máo, nǐ gěi bāshí'èr kuài ba.
店主： 一共 八十二块 四 毛，你给八十二块 吧。

Mǎdīng: Wǒ méi dài shǒujī, gěi nǐ xiànjīn ba.
马丁： 我 没带手机，给你现金 吧。

Diànzhǔ: Xíng!
店主： 行！

Mǎdīng: Zhè shì bāshísān kuài, búyòng zhǎo le.
马丁： 这是 八十三 块，不用 找 了。

Diànzhǔ: Zhǎo nǐ liù máo.
店主： 找 你六 毛。

Mǎdīng: Suànle ba.
马丁： 算了吧。

Diànzhǔ: Bù, wǒ yǒu língqián.
店主： 不，我 有 零钱。

How much are the grapes

(In the fruit store)

Storekeeper: Hello! What would you like?

Martin: How much are the grapes?

Storekeeper: Twenty-eight *yuan* half a kilo.

Martin: It's so expensive.

Storekeeper: Yes. This kind of grapes is imported from abroad, the domestic ones are cheaper.

Martin: Are they sweet?

Storekeeper: Both of these two kinds are very sweet. You can try them.

Martin: (Tasting one) Ah, they are so sweet. I'd like some. I want the cheaper ones.

Storekeeper: Is there anything else you want to buy?

Martin: How much is half a kilo of strawberries?

Storekeeper: Fifteen *yuan* half a kilo.

Martin: And some strawberries and some kiwis.

Storekeeper: How many kiwis do you want?

Martin: Five, please.

Storekeeper: That's eighty-two *yuan* and four *jiao*. Just give me eighty-two *yuan*.

Martin: I don't have my cell phone with me. I'll pay you in cash.

Storekeeper: All right!

Martin: Here's eighty-three *yuan* and keep the change.

Storekeeper: Here's 6 *jiao* for you.

Martin: Forget it.

Storekeeper: No, I have changes here.

二 生词 New Words

1	葡萄	pútao	名	grape
2	卖	mài	动	to sell
3	店主	diànzhǔ	名	storekeeper
4	来	lái	动	*used as a substitute for a verb so as to avoid repetition*
5	块（元）	kuài (yuán)	量	*yuan* (*the monetary unit of China*)
6	斤	jīn	量	*jin* (*a traditional unit of weight, equivalent to 1/2 kilogram*)
7	贵	guì	形	expensive
8	种	zhǒng	量	kind; type; sort
9	外国	wàiguó	名	foreign country
10	进口	jìnkǒu	动	to import
11	国产	guóchǎn	形	domestic
12	便宜	piányi	形	cheap
13	特	tè	副	very; especially
14	要	yào	动	to want
15	草莓	cǎoméi	名	strawberry

16 钱	qián	名	money
17 猕猴桃	míhóutáo	名	kiwi
18 毛（角）	máo (jiǎo)	量	*jiao* (*the monetary unit of China*)
19 带	dài	动	to bring with
20 现金	xiànjīn	名	cash
21 不用	búyòng	副	need not
22 找	zhǎo	动	to give change
23 算了	suànle	动	to forget it
24 零钱	língqián	名	change

三 注释 Notes

（一）人民币

人民币有以下面值：

There are the following denominations in RMB:

一角、五角、一元、五元、十元、二十元、五十元、一百元。

One *jiao*, five *jiao*, one *yuan*, five *yuan*, ten *yuan*, twenty yuan, fifty *yuan* and one hundred *yuan*.

（二）……吧 The modal particle “吧”

表示要求、商量的语气。例如：

The modal particle “吧” may express a tone of demand, request or consultation, e.g.,

1. 来点吧。
2. 好吧。

（三）“二”+量词 → 两（liǎng）+量词 “二”(→“两”) + measure word

“二”在量词前常读成“liǎng”，写作“两”。例如：

When “二” is used before a measure word, it is usually replaced by “两 (liǎng)” , e.g.,

两个猕猴桃　　两个人　　两斤
* 二个猕猴桃　　* 二个人　　二斤

(四) “几” 和 “多少” “几” and “多少”

询问者估计数量在 1 ～ 10 之间时，用 “几”；估计在 10 以上或难以估计时，用 “多少”。例如：

When the amount is estimated to be between 1 and 10, “几” is used; when it is more than 10 or hard to be estimated, “多少” is used, e.g.,

1. A：你家有几口人？
   B：我家有五口人。
2. A：你们班有多少个学生？
   B：十八个。

四 练习 Exercises

(一) 朗读 Read aloud

1. 读出下列的数 Read out the following numbers

31 32 33 34 35 36 37 38 39 40
41 42 43 44 45 46 47 48 49 50
51 52 53 54 55 56 57 58 59 60
61……………………………………100

百	十	个
		8
	7	1
	8	9
	9	9
1	0	0

yì	qiānwàn	bǎiwàn	shíwàn	wàn	qiān	bǎi	shí	gè
14	1	1	7	8	0	0	0	0

2. 朗读下列发音相近的词语 Read aloud the following words and expressions with similar pronunciation

pútao 葡萄	fǔdǎo 辅导	shuǐguǒ 水果	shuǐhuò 水货
tè tián 特甜	tè xián 特咸	cǎoméi 草莓	dǎoméi 倒霉
suànle 算了	sàn le 散了	língqián 零钱	lǐng qián 领钱

3. 朗读下列带半三声的词语 Read aloud the following words with the half 3rd tones

Běijīng 北京	měi tiān 每天	hǎochī 好吃	wǎncān 晚餐
yǐqián 以前	yǔyán 语言	kěnéng 可能	lǚxíng 旅行
fǔdǎo 辅导	xǐ zǎo 洗澡	kǒuyǔ 口语	kěyǐ 可以

4. 朗读下列带儿化韵的词语 Read aloud the following words and expressions with the *r*-ending retroflexion

xiǎoháir 小孩儿	hǎowánr 好玩儿	méi shìr 没事儿	liáo tiānr 聊天儿
yìdiǎnr 一点儿	yíxiàr 一下儿	yíhuìr 一会儿	yíkuàir 一块儿
yǒudiǎnr 有点儿	miàntiáor 面条儿	chàng gēr 唱歌儿	huà huàr 画画儿

（二）**看图会话** Look at the pictures and practice the conversation

A：________怎么卖 / 多少钱一斤？

B：________。

 xiāngjiāo bananas 4.5 元 / 斤	 píngguǒ apples 6 元 / 斤	 júzi oranges 8 元 / 斤
 xīguā a watermelon 2 元 / 斤	 lí pears 6 元 / 斤	 yīngtao cherries 22 元 / 斤
 lìzhī lychees 16 元 / 斤		

（三）**替换并朗读** Replace and read aloud

1. A：你好！来点儿什么？
   B：葡萄怎么卖？

苹果	橘子	草莓
猕猴桃	梨	桃

2. A：还买别的吗？
   B：草莓一斤多少钱？

苹果	橘子	葡萄
猕猴桃	梨	桃

3. A：再来一些草莓和几个猕猴桃吧。
B：一共八十二块六毛。

苹果	梨
葡萄	苹果
橘子	梨
香蕉	西红柿

（四）**选词填空并朗读下列句子** Choose the appropriate words to fill in the blanks and read aloud the following sentences

几　多少

1. A：你家有________口人？
B：我家有五口人。
2. A：现在________点？
B：现在九点半。
3. A：你今天有________节课？
B：我今天有四节课。
4. A：你们班有________人？
B：我们班有十八个人。
5. A：葡萄________钱一斤？
B：二十八元一斤。

怎么　进口　便宜　再　一共　买　甜　斤

1. 你想________点儿什么？
2. A：葡萄________卖？
B：二十八块一________。
3. 这种葡萄是外国________的，国产的便宜一些。
4. A：这两种葡萄都特________，你可以尝尝。
B：啊，真甜。来点儿吧，我要________的。

5. A：还买别的吗？

B：________来一些草莓和猕猴桃吧。

6. ________八十二块六毛，你给八十二吧。

（五）完成下列会话并大声朗读 Complete the following conversations and read them aloud

A：葡萄怎么卖？

B：________________________________。

A：怎么这么贵？

B：________________________________。

A：甜吗？

B：________________________________。

（六）根据实际情况回答问题 Answer the questions according to the actual situations

1. 你常买水果吗？
2. 你常吃什么水果？
3. 你们那儿的水果便宜吗？
4. 你们那儿的草莓 / 苹果 / 橘子 / 香蕉 / 西瓜 / 梨多少钱一斤？
5. 你觉得这里的东西贵不贵？

（七）和同学一起表演课文 Act out the text with your classmates

（八）读后说 Read the passage and say it

我去买水果，店主问我今天想来点儿什么，我问他葡萄怎么卖，他说一斤二十八块。我觉得有点儿贵。他说这种葡萄是外国进口的，国产的便宜一些。

我买了一些便宜的葡萄，还买了一些草莓和几个猕猴桃，一共花了八十多块钱。

(九) 怎么表达 How to express

bǎozhèng
保证 promising

Wǒ bǎozhèng shuō dào zuò dào.
1. 我 保证 说 到 做 到。

I assure you I'll do what I said.

Wǒ jué bú zuò rènhé duìbuqǐ nǐ de shìr.
2. 我 决 不 做 任何 对不起 你 的 事儿。

I shall never do any disservice to you.

(十) 朗读中国经典诗词，请注意语音语调 Read aloud the classic Chinese poem and pay attention to the pronunciation and intonation

Méihuā
梅花

[Sòng] Wáng Ānshí
[宋] 王 安石（1021—1086）

Qiángjiǎo shù zhī méi, líng hán dúzì kāi.
墙角 数 枝 梅，凌 寒 独 自 开。
Yáo zhī bú shì xuě, wèi yǒu àn xiāng lái.
遥 知 不 是 雪，为 有 暗 香 来。

(十一) 请欣赏下列著名的词句 Please enjoy the following well-known saying

Mǎimai bù chéng rényì zài.
买卖 不 成 仁义在。

Benevolence and uprightness should exist between buyer and seller even if they fail to clinch a deal.

Mǎi mài gōngpíng, tóng sǒu wú qī.
买 卖 公平， 童 叟 无 欺。

Be fair in buying and selling, and cheat neither the old nor the young.

词汇表 Vocabulary

A	啊	à	叹	(*used to express admiration or surprise*) ah; O; oh	6
	啊	a	助	*used at the end of a sentence to express agreement, defensiveness, urge, etc.*	5
	哎呀	āiyā	叹	(*used to express surprise*) wow; gee; my	14
	爱	ài	动	to love	1
B	八	bā	数	eight	1
	把	bǎ	量	*for something with a handle*	13
	爸爸	bàba	名	father	1
	吧	ba	助	*used at the end of an imperative sentence to soften the tone*	6
	白	bái	形	white	14
	棒	bàng	形	great; excellent	9
	包子	bāozi	名	steamed stuffed bun	6
	杯	bēi	名、量	cup	11
	比较	bǐjiào	副、动	rather; relatively; to compare	12
	遍	biàn	量	(*for actions*) once through; one time	7
	别	bié	副	don't	8
	不错	búcuò	形	not bad	15
	不用	búyòng	副	need not	16
	不	bù	副	no	5
	布置	bùzhì	动	to assign	7
C	才	cái	副	not ... until; then and only then; only when	3
	草莓	cǎoméi	名	strawberry	16
	茶	chá	名	tea	6

尝	cháng	动	to taste	6
常	cháng	副	often	11
吃	chī	动	to eat	6
吃苦	chī kǔ	动	to suffer hardships	8
窗口	chuāngkǒu	名	window	13
从	cóng	介	from	13
错	cuò	形	wrong	15
D				
打	dǎ	动	to phone	13
大	dà	形	big; large	1
大家	dàjiā	代	everyone	7
大夫	dàifu	名	doctor	14
带	dài	动	to bring with	16
但	dàn	连	but	9
当然	dāngrán	副	of course	13
倒	dào	动	to pour	6
得	de	助	*used between a verb or an adjective and its complement to indicate the result or degree*	9
弟弟	dìdi	名	younger brother	4
电话	diànhuà	名	phone	13
店主	diànzhǔ	名	storekeeper	16
懂	dǒng	动	to understand	7
都	dōu	副	all; both	4
读	dú	动	to read	7
对	duì	形	right; correct	2
多	duō	数、形	(*used after numerals*) more than; many; much	5
多少	duōshao	代	how many; how much	5
E				
饿	è	形	hungry	6
儿子	érzi	名	son	8

	二	èr	数	two	5
	二胡	èrhú	名	*erhu* (two-stringed bowed instrument with a low register)	15
G	刚	gāng	副	just	13
	高铁	gāotiě	名	high-speed railway	12
	高兴	gāoxìng	形	happy	13
	哥哥	gēge	名	elder brother	4
	给	gěi	动	to give	11
	给	gěi	介	(*used to introduce the recipient of an action*) for; to	13
	跟	gēn	介、动	with; to follow	4
	工作	gōngzuò	名、动	job; to work	14
	公园	gōngyuán	名	park	5
	狗	gǒu	名	dog	4
	古老	gǔlǎo	形	ancient; old	12
	贵	guì	形	valuable; precious	3
	贵	guì		honorable	13
	贵	guì	形	expensive	16
	贵姓	guìxìng	名	one's (honorable) surname	13
	国产	guóchǎn	形	domestic	16
H	哈	hā	拟声	ha; ha-ha (*sound of laughing with the mouth wide open, usu. reduplicated*)	4
	还	hái	副	still	13
	还	hái	副	also; too	15
	还是	háishi	连	or	11
	汉语	Hànyǔ	名	Chinese (language)	2
	汉字	Hànzì	名	Chinese character	12
	好	hǎo	形	good; well; fine	1
	好	hǎo	形	easy (to do)	13
	好吃	hǎochī	形	delicious	6

好喝	hǎohē	形	good to drink	6
号	hào	名	number	13
和	hé	形	harmonious; peaceful; kind; gentle	3
和	hé	连	and	12
和平	hépíng	名	peace	3
黑板	hēibǎn	名	blackboard	7
很	hěn	副	very	4
红茶	hóngchá	名	black tea	11
互相	hùxiāng	副	each other	4
护士	hùshi	名	nurse	14
画	huà	动	to draw; to paint	15
画儿	huàr	名	drawing; painting	15
会	huì	动	to be able to	12
J 机	jī		machine	10
几	jǐ	代	how many	5
加	jiā	动	to add	13
家	jiā	名	family; home	1
简单	jiǎndān	形	simple	12
交	jiāo	动	to associate with; to befriend	13
饺子	jiǎozi	名	Chinese dumpling	6
叫	jiào	动	to call; to name	13
接	jiē	动	to catch	13
节	jié	量	*a measure word for lessons*	5
姐姐	jiějie	名	elder sister	4
介绍	jièshào	动	to introduce	10
斤	jīn	量	*jin* (*a traditional unit of weight, equivalent to 1/2 kilogram*)	16
今天	jīntiān	名	today	5
进	jìn	动	to come in	7
进口	jìnkǒu	动	to import	16

九	jiǔ	数	nine	5
就	jiù	副	if that is the case, then	9
就	jiù	副	exactly; precisely	12
觉得	juéde	动	to feel; to think	9
K 咖啡	kāfēi	名	coffee	11
看	kàn	动	to look; to watch	7
看	kàn	动	to think; to consider	10
可	kě	副	*used in a declarative sentence for emphasis*	11
可能	kěnéng	副	possibly; probably	14
可是	kě shì		*used for emphasis*	11
可以	kěyǐ	能动	may; can	13
课	kè	名	lesson; course	5
课文	kèwén	名	text	7
苦	kǔ	形	bitter; painful	8
块（元）	kuài (yuán)	量	*yuan* (*the monetary unit of China*)	16
快	kuài	副	hurry up	13
快乐	kuàilè	形	happy	15
L 拉	lā	动	to play (a musical instrument)	15
来	lái	动	to come	9
来	lái	动	*used as a substitute for a verb so as to avoid repetition*	16
蓝	lán	形	blue	14
老师	lǎoshī	名	teacher	3
零钱	língqián	名	change	16
留学	liú xué	动	to study abroad	8
留学生	liúxuéshēng	名	overseas student	13
六	liù	数	six	5
楼	lóu	名	tower; storeyed building	13
楼下	lóu xià		downstairs	13

	路	lù	名	way; road	13
	旅行	lǚxíng	动	to travel	8
	绿茶	lǜchá	名	green tea	11
M	妈妈	māma	名	mother	1
	吗	ma	助	*used at the end of an interrogative sentence*	4
	嘛	ma	助	*indicating that something is obvious*	13
	买	mǎi	动	to buy	6
	卖	mài	动	to sell	16
	慢	màn	形	slow	7
	忙	máng	形	busy	8
	毛（角）	máo (jiǎo)	量	*jiao (the monetary unit of China)*	16
	没（有）	méi (yǒu)	动、副	not to have; not	12
	没问题	méi wèntí		no problem	12
	每	měi	代	every; each; per	15
	每天	měi tiān		every day	15
	美	měi	形	beautiful	3
	妹妹	mèimei	名	younger sister	4
	们	men	后缀	*used after a personal pronoun or a noun to show plural number*	4
	猕猴桃	míhóutáo	名	kiwi	16
	名字	míngzi	名	name; first name	13
	明	míng		bright	12
	明亮	míngliàng	形	bright	12
N	拿	ná	动	to take	13
	哪里	nǎlǐ	代	*used when responding politely to a compliment*	15
	那	nà	代	that; those	6
	那边	nàbiān	代	there	14
	奶奶	nǎinai	名	grandmother	1
	难	nán	形	difficult	8

呢	ne	助	*used at the end of a declarative sentence to reinforce the assertion or play up the effect of exaggeration*	5
能	néng	助动	can; to be able to	2
你	nǐ	代	you	1
你们	nǐmen	代	you (plural)	4
您	nín	代	you (honorific)	7
努力	nǔlì	形	hard-working	15
女儿	nǚ'ér	名	daughter	8
P 怕	pà	动	to be afraid of	8
拍	pāi	动	to take (a picture); to shoot	10
朋友	péngyou	名	friend	10
琵琶	pípa	名	*pipa* (Chinese string musical instrument with a fretted fingerboard historically with a plectrum, but now mainly with the fingers)	15
屏幕	píngmù	名	screen	7
便宜	piányi	形	cheap	16
葡萄	pútao	名	grape	16
普洱茶	pǔ'ěrchá	名	Pu'er tea	6
Q 七	qī	数	seven	5
钱	qián	名	money	16
请	qǐng	动	please	7
请问	qǐngwèn	动	excuse me	13
去	qù	动	to go; to leave	5
R 人生	rénshēng	名	life	3
认识	rènshi	动	to know	12
扔	rēng	动	to throw	13
容易	róngyì	形	easy	9
S 三	sān	数	three	5
善	shàn	形	kind-hearted; good; virtuous	3

上课	shàng kè	动	to give a lesson	7
上午	shàngwǔ	名	morning	15
什么	shénme	代	what	6
生词	shēngcí	名	new word	7
十	shí	数	ten	5
世界	shìjiè	名	world	3
事儿	shìr	名	thing; matter; affair	13
视频	shìpín	名	video	4
是	shì	动	to be (am, is, are, etc.)	6
手	shǒu	名	hand	10
手机	shǒujī	名	mobile phone	10
书法	shūfǎ	名	calligraphy	15
叔叔	shūshu	名	uncle	8
谁	shéi	代	who; whom	13
说	shuō	动	to speak; to talk	7
四	sì	数	four	5
算了	suànle	动	to forget it	16
T				
他	tā	代	he; him	4
它	tā	代	it	4
它们	tāmen	代	they	12
她	tā	代	she; her	4
太	tài	副	too; extremely; much too	8
太阳	tàiyáng	名	sun	12
弹	tán	动	to play (a musical instrument)	15
特	tè	副	very; especially	16
天	tiān	名	day	15
天下	tiānxià	名	the whole country or the world	2
甜	tián	形	sweet	8
听	tīng	动	to listen	7
挺	tǐng	副	very; rather; quite	8

通过	tōngguò	介	by means of; via	4
同学	tóngxué	名	schoolmate; classmate	7
图片	túpiàn	名	photograph	12
W 外国	wàiguó	名	foreign country	16
外贸	wàimào	名	foreign trade	13
微信	wēixìn	名	WeChat	13
为	wéi	动	to be; to mean; to act as	3
问候	wènhòu	动	to ask after	4
问题	wèntí	名	question; problem	12
我	wǒ	代	I; me	1
我们	wǒmen	代	we; us	4
五	wǔ	数	five	1
X 喜欢	xǐhuan	动	to like; to be fond of	11
下	xià	名	low position or rank	13
下午	xiàwǔ	名	afternoon	15
现代	xiàndài	形	modern	13
现金	xiànjīn	名	cash	16
现在	xiànzài	名	now	7
想	xiǎng	动	to want	6
像	xiàng	动	to be like	12
些	xiē	量	some; a few	6
写	xiě	动	to write	12
星期	xīngqī	名	week	5
行	xíng	动	to go; to travel	2
幸福	xìngfú	形	happy	3
姓	xìng	名	surname	13
熊猫	xióngmāo	名	panda	7
学	xué	动	to study; to learn	2
学生	xuéshēng	名	student	3

	学习	xuéxí	动	to study; to learn	2
	学校	xuéxiào	名	school	5
Y	呀	ya	助	*used instead of* 啊 *after a syllable ending in* a, e, i, *or*, ü	12
	眼光	yǎnguāng	名	eye; sight; vision	8
	要	yào	动	to need	3
	要	yào	动	to want	16
	钥匙	yàoshi	名	key	13
	爷爷	yéye	名	grandfather	1
	也	yě	副	too; also	4
	一	yī	数	one	1
	医生	yīshēng	名	doctor	14
	一下儿	yíxiàr		(*used after a verb as its complement, indicating an act or an attempt*) one time	10
	一点儿	yìdiǎnr		a little; a bit; some	6
	一起	yìqǐ	副	together	5
	意思	yìsi	名	interest; fun	12
	英语	Yīngyǔ	名	English	7
	应该	yīnggāi	能动	should; ought to	3
	用	yòng	动	to use	10
	有	yǒu	动	to have	5
	有点儿	yǒudiǎnr	副	somewhat; rather; a bit	6
	有意思	yǒu yìsi		interesting; enjoyable	12
	预习	yùxí	动	(of students) to prepare lessons before class	7
	月亮	yuèliang	名	moon	12
Z	再	zài	副	again	7
	在	zài	副	*used to indicate an action in progress*	11
	咱们	zánmen	代	we	12
	怎么	zěnme	代	how	7

怎么样	zěnmeyàng	代	how about	3
怎样	zěnyàng	代	how	3
找	zhǎo	动	to look for; to try to find	12
找	zhǎo	动	to give change	16
照相	zhào xiàng	动	to take a picture	10
这	zhè	代	this; these	6
这儿	zhèr	代	here	14
这些	zhèxiē	代	these	6
真	zhēn	形	true; real; genuine	3
真正	zhēnzhèng	形	real	11
争气	zhēng qì	动	to make effort to seek self-improvement	15
正	zhèng	副	just; right; exactly	14
知道	zhīdào	动	to know; to be aware of	9
只	zhǐ	副	only	15
志气	zhìqì	名	aspiration; ambition	15
中	zhōng	名	inside	8
中文	Zhōngwén	名	Chinese (language)	13
种	zhǒng	量	kind; type; sort	16
周	zhōu	名	week	15
周末	zhōumò	名	weekend	12
住	zhù	动	*used as a complement after a verb, indicating a steadiness or firmness*	13
专业	zhuānyè	名	major; speciality	13
追求	zhuīqiú	动	to seek; to pursue; to go after	3
桌子	zhuōzi	名	table; desk	13
走	zǒu	动	to walk; to go	13
作业	zuòyè	名	homework	7
坐	zuò	动	to sit	7
做	zuò	动	to do	8

专名 Proper Nouns

华为	Huáwéi	Huawei	14
李大同	Lǐ Dàtóng	a name of person	13
马丁	Mǎdīng	a name of person	13
玛丽	Mǎlì	Mary	4
美国	Měiguó	U.S.A	13
苹果	Píngguǒ	Apple	14
西湖	Xī Hú	West Lake (one of China's most famous lakes in Hangzhou)	11
谢钟文	Xiè Zhōngwén	a name of person	13
长城	Chángchéng	the Great Wall	12
中国	Zhōngguó	China	8